Cambridge First Certificate
Examination Practice 4

Cambridge First Certificate

Examination Practice 4

*University of Cambridge
Local Examinations Syndicate*

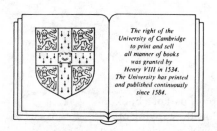

The right of the
University of Cambridge
to print and sell
all manner of books
was granted by
Henry VIII in 1534.
The University has printed
and published continuously
since 1584.

Cambridge University Press
Cambridge
New York   Port Chester
Melbourne   Sydney

1051647 6

Published by the Press Syndicate of the University of Cambridge
The Pitt Building, Trumpington Street, Cambridge CB2 1RP
40 West 20th Street, New York, NY 10011–4211, USA
10 Stamford Road, Oakleigh, Melbourne 3166, Australia

© Cambridge University Press 1991

First published 1991

Printed in Great Britain at the University Press, Cambridge

ISBN 0 521 40834 2 Student's Book
ISBN 0 521 40735 4 Teacher's Book
ISBN 0 521 40733 8 Set of 2 cassettes

GO

Contents

Acknowledgements

To the student   1

Practice Test 1   2

Practice Test 2   24

Practice Test 3   44

Practice Test 4   64

Practice Test 5   83

Interview Exercises   101

Sample Answer Sheets   121

Acknowledgements

The authors and publishers are grateful to the following for permission to reproduce texts and illustrations. It has not been possible to identify sources of all the material used and in such cases the publishers would welcome information from copyright owners.

Curtis Brown Ltd on behalf of John Wain, for the extract on pp. 4–5 from *A Visit at Tea Time* in *Death of the Hind Legs and Other Stories* by John Wain, © John Wain 1963; Harpers and Queen and Caroline Clifton Mogg for the extract from *A Loom with a View* on pp. 5–6; The Observer for the extract from *The Observer Guide to European Cookery* by Jane Grigson on p. 7; APV Anda for the Airstream Air Filter advertisement on p. 8; David Crystal for the passage on pp. 26–27; William Heinemann Ltd, The Bodley Head Ltd and the Estate of Graham Greene for the extract on pp. 46–47 from *I Spy* in *Collected Stories* by Graham Greene; The Observer for the extract from *Journey into the Interior* by Rodney Tyler on pp. 66–67; The Times for the extract from *Drive to Simplify Official Language* by Robin Young on p. 69, © Times Newspapers Ltd 1981; Express Newspapers plc for the extract from *Born in New York* on p. 87; IPC Magazines Ltd for the travel feature on p. 88, extracted from Woman's Realm Magazine, © IPC Magazines 1986; David Argent for the first photograph on p. 101; Nina Hajnal for the photographs on pp. 101 (lower), 102, 107 and 108; Paul Popper Ltd for the photographs on pp. 104 (lower), 105, 110, 111, 112 and 116; Jeremy Pembrey for the photograph on p. 113; Longman Group Ltd for the illustrations on p. 117; Longman Group Ltd and Hamish Hamilton for the extracts from *The Go-Between* by L. P. Hartley on p. 118.

To the student

This book is for candidates preparing for the University of Cambridge First Certificate in English examination and provides practice in all the written and oral papers. It contains 5 complete tests. The written papers are all based on the First Certificate examinations set in 1988 and 1989, and the oral paper, Paper 5, is based on more recent First Certificate examinations. The examination consists of 5 papers as follows:

Paper 1 Reading Comprehension (1 hour)
   Section A consists of 25 multiple-choice items in the form of a sentence with a blank to be filled in by 1 of 4 words or phrases.
   Section B consists of 15 multiple-choice items based on 3 or more reading passages of different types.

Paper 2 Composition (1½ hours)
   There are 5 topics from which you choose 2. The range of topics includes a letter, a description, a narrative, a discursive composition or a speech. There is also a topic based on optional reading. (In these books the questions based on optional reading are set on the kind of books that are prescribed each year. These are *not* the actual books prescribed for any particular year; they are just given as examples.)

Paper 3 Use of English (2 hours)
   There are exercises of various kinds which test your control of English usage and grammatical structure. There is also a directed writing exercise where you study a text often containing an illustration, map or diagram, from which you must extract the required information and present it in a coherent form.

Paper 4 Listening Comprehension (20 to 30 minutes)
   You answer a variety of questions on recorded passages (normally 4) from English broadcasts, interviews, announcements, phone messages and conversations. Each passage is heard twice.

Paper 5 Interview (about 15 minutes)
   You take part in a theme-based conversation with the examiner. Photographs, extracts from authentic materials and problem solving activities, all linked by theme, are used to stimulate the discussion. You may take Paper 5 alone or with one or two other candidates and you may, if you wish, talk about one of the optional reading texts.

Practice Test 1

PAPER 1   READING COMPREHENSION   (1 hour)

Answer all questions. Indicate your choice of answer in every case **on the separate answer sheet** *already given out, which should show your name and examination index number. Follow carefully the instructions about how to record your answers. Give* **one answer only** *to each question. Marks will not be deducted for wrong answers: your total score on this test will be the number of correct answers you give.*

SECTION A

In this section you must choose the word or phrase which best completes each sentence. **On your answer sheet** *indicate the letter A, B, C or D against the number of each item 1 to 25 for the word or phrase you choose.*

1 She can't get home .... she has no money.
   A unless   B if   C until   D without

2 The water company will have to .... off water supplies while repairs to the pipes are carried out.
   A cut   B take   C break   D set

3 If you're not too tired we could have a .... of tennis after lunch.
   A match   B play   C game   D party

4 .... accepting your job offer, I'd like to know a bit more about the company.
   A In advance   B In order   C Until   D Before

5 Can you .... the papers with you when you come to see me, please?
   A bring   B collect   C take   D get

6 Can you tell me the .... of these shoes?
   A charge   B price   C amount   D expense

7 I don't feel well – but I don't know what's the matter .... me.
   A of   B for   C to   D with

8 It is too early in the .... to expect many visitors to the town.
   A term   B season   C time   D calendar

9 .... is a complete mystery how they ever got there in that car.
   A There   B That   C It   D This

10 I love this painting of an old man. He has such a beautiful, ... smile.
   A childhood   B childish   C childless   D childlike

11 If you wish to take photographs you'll have to have ....
   A an application   B a permit   C an allowance   D an admission

12 Come ...., children! Get your coats on or you'll be late for school.
   A to   B across   C along   D over

13 She tried to prevent the dog .... running into the road.
   A from   B to   C against   D for

14 My main .... to the new bypass is that it will spoil the countryside.
   A object   B objection   C objective   D objecting

15 You'd better leave for the airport now .... there's a lot of traffic on the way.
   A in fact   B in time   C in order   D in case

16 He has just bought .... expensive new furniture.
   A an   B some   C these   D those

17 Because it had not rained for several months, there was a .... of water.
   A shortage   B drop   C scarce   D waste

18 I should like to thank you, ... my colleagues, for the welcome you have given us.
   A on account of   B on behalf of   C because of   D instead of

19 It's very dry today. Will you help me .... the plants?
   A moisten   B wet   C water   D sprinkle

20 It's no use .... a language if you don't try to speak it too.
   A to learn   B learned   C learning   D learn

21 The doctor told him to keep .... sweets and chocolate to lose weight.
   A at   B back   C up   D off

22 As long as they .... stay for more than a few days, they can sleep at my flat.
   A don't   B didn't   C shan't   D wouldn't

23 According .... the map we should take the next turning on the left.
   A to   B as   C on   D by

24 Would you please be kind enough to .... me to the station?
   A aim   B turn   C direct   D signal

25 Don't forget our appointment. You'd better put it in your ....
   A agenda   B diary   C calendar   D directory

SECTION B

*In this section you will find after each of the passages a number of questions or
unfinished statements about the passage, each with four suggested answers or ways of
finishing. You must choose the one which you think fits best according to the passage.*
On your answer sheet, *indicate the letter A, B, C or D against the number of each
item 26–40 for the answer you choose. Give* **one answer only** *to each question. Read
each passage right through before choosing your answers.*

FIRST PASSAGE

Williams had to turn back halfway down the drive. His mouth was dry and his
heart had begun to beat very loudly. He went out through the gate again and
stood by the hedge, out of sight of the house. If anyone happened to be
watching through a window, he did not want to be seen behaving in an
unusual way.

'It's perfectly reasonable,' he said out loud. Thinking aloud was an old habit
of his, but in this case he comforted himself with the thought that it was only
natural to try out his voice before ringing the bell. 'It's quite reasonable,' he
repeated. 'Why shouldn't I want to see it? I shall not be putting them to much
trouble. And after fifteen years . . .'

It occurred to him that, even standing in the shelter of the hedge, he could still
be seen from the attic window. How many autumn afternoons, exactly like this
one, had he spent behind that window. 'Why do you spend so much time in the
attic?' he could hear his mother saying. She felt it was ungrateful of him, after
they had given up one of the downstairs rooms and made it into his play-room,
that he played there so little, preferring the high, secret attic, so much better for
dreaming. The play-room was a challenge to activity with its electric railway
system, its boxes of toys and puzzles and the bright pictures on its walls. Only
in the attic had he felt free to imagine his own world and live in it for hours at a
time.

Fifteen years – surely that gave him the right to go up to the front door, ring
the bell and make a simple request? Setting his shoulders back, he turned
quickly into the drive and walked the whole way up to the front door.

When he pressed the bell he heard nothing. For a moment his nervousness threatened to come back, at the thought that the bell might be out of order, which would present him with the choice of either using the knocker or standing there until someone discovered him by accident. But he pulled himself together before his control began to slip. It was a big house and the bell rang in a distant room, probably with at least two shut doors between it and the front entrance. He had a sudden mental picture of the interior of the house and in particular of the kitchen: warm and bright and Frances setting out the tea-things.

26   He turned back when he was halfway down the drive because he
    A   felt too nervous to continue.
    B   wasn't sure if it was the right house.
    C   felt thirsty.
    D   wanted to see if anyone was watching him.

27   Williams had preferred the attic to the play-room because
    A   his mother told him not to play there.
    B   he liked looking out of the attic window.
    C   the toys in the attic were more interesting.
    D   he could lose himself there in his own thoughts.

28   Why did he go to the house?
    A   to see some old friends
    B   to look round the house again
    C   to see his mother again
    D   to collect his old toys

29   He wasn't sure the bell had rung because
    A   it was a large house.
    B   he hadn't pressed it hard enough.
    C   it wasn't working.
    D   the front door was closed.

SECOND PASSAGE

Just inside the walls of Florence stands a factory where silk is handwoven on machines that date back to the fifteenth century. The factory, successful at the height of silk production in the eighteenth century, was almost unknown in the twentieth century until it was rescued about seven years ago by the Marchese Pucci, whose name has for so long been associated with beautiful and luxurious silks. Once again the factory is producing some of the most beautiful and expensive handwoven silks in the world. Expensive they may be, but these silks are very strong, and the quality and colours are such that the cloth woven here will last at least one lifetime – probably several.

The originator of all this beauty, the silkworm, is a sensitive little creature, living only on the freshly gathered and chopped leaves of the white mulberry. It is so nervous that loud noises, strong smells, or even the threat of thunder can kill it, so it is not entirely surprising that silkworm farming is so rarely practised in Britain today. In fact there have been several attempts, over the centuries, to start silkworm farming in England, but few of them have been successful. For example there was the attempt of James I who, though anxious to build up the silk industry, made a bad mistake and planted the black mulberry instead of the white. An easy error, and one that only the silkworms objected to.

Although some silk is still grown in Italy, the Po valley, for example, is no longer covered by mulberry trees as it once was. The silk for the factory is sent raw from China – a journey almost as slow as it was in the second century. It is then dyed before being delivered to the Florentine building where it sits on the worn tiles waiting to be woven into bright butterfly-coloured cloth. The silk is protected from the light by protective cotton curtains. The patterns for the fabrics are made by using heavy cards which have holes in different designs, and allow selected lengths of silk through the holes, whilst rejecting others, thereby forming the designs, which vary greatly when the cloth is finished.

30   What is special about the silk factory described in the passage?
    A   It has been famous since the eighteenth century.
    B   It uses very old machines.
    C   It was closed for 200 years.
    D   It has always been owned by the Pucci family.

31   The silk that is woven there is
    A   cheap and strong.
    B   expensive and long-lasting.
    C   cheap and colourful.
    D   delicate and long-lasting.

32   Why did James I's attempt to start silkworm farming fail?
    A   The mulberry trees would not grow in England.
    B   The countryside was too noisy.
    C   The silkworms were given the wrong food.
    D   It was too cold in England.

33   What happens to the silk when it reaches the factory?
    A   It is dyed.
    B   It is mixed with cotton.
    C   It is woven into a pattern.
    D   It is sorted into different lengths.

THIRD PASSAGE

Food and ideas about cooking it have been passing from one part of the world to another ever since the stone age revolution began in the Middle East. They were part of the spread of civilisation, though since people change their tastes in painting and architecture much faster than their tastes in food, knowledge of what was eaten is far less than knowledge of the houses that were lived in or the clothes that were worn. Cookery books were few before the 17th century – and how close are the general eating habits at any period to the cookery books published?

Change owed more to the movement of people, of armies, of merchants, of wealthy landowners, than to books. Before canals, the railways, good roads, most people ate what could be produced within a thirty-mile area. Ports did better, of course, if they were on a big trade route. For most people food was basically regional food and there was not always enough of it either. Even in good areas, poor country people had little to eat since most of what they produced went for sale at local markets. Only wealthy men could buy expensive seeds to grow unusual vegetables, or employ gardeners who understood how to grow fine fruit unfamiliar to the place they lived in, or afford cooks trained elsewhere to provide variety at mealtimes.

The undoubted advantages of present-day large-scale manufacture and organisation – outstanding cleanliness, quick distribution, prices that allow far more people than ever in the past to satisfy their hunger – have not so far come to us together with an excellent quality of flavour. Moreover, in a world where possibilities are endless, business seems to try to limit choice beyond a certain level. Of the 300 varieties of pear that are listed by one French 17th century gardener – even though he had to admit that only 30 of them were really worth eating – only about half a dozen are now produced in Europe.

34   Why do we know so little about the food people ate in the past?
    A   Eating habits used to change very quickly.
    B   There were no cookery books before the 17th century.
    C   Cookery books probably don't reflect contemporary eating habits.
    D   There are very few paintings of food.

35   Changes in eating habits were due to
    A   shortages of basic foods.
    B   the influence of travellers.
    C   developments in agriculture.
    D   the recipes of foreign cooks.

36   What is the problem with our food today?
    A   It's too expensive for many people.
    B   It's manufactured too quickly.
    C   It doesn't taste as it used to.
    D   It's exported in very large quantities.

37   What point is the author making in the example about the pear in the last
     paragraph?
     A   There is not as much variety now as before.
     B   There was more variety in the past but quality was not as high.
     C   Most pears which were produced were inedible.
     D   There is more variety outside Europe than in Europe.

FOURTH PASSAGE

BE HEALTHY, WEALTHY & WISE

Clean Your Air with **AIRSTREAM**

HEALTHY:

Smoke, pollution and housedust are responsible for many illnesses — AIRSTREAM filters all these from the air.

WEALTHY:

Save money on heating and decorating costs, don't throw heated air out of the window, clean it. Walls and ceilings attract dust and smoke particles by a sort of electricity; filtering the air usually doubles the time before redecoration is necessary.

WISE:

Choose AIRSTREAM 100, the safe way to clean your air. AIRSTREAM filters out particles down to 0.01 microns in size, a strand of your hair is about 50 microns in diameter. AIRSTREAM can be fixed on wall or ceiling and is suitable for rooms up to 3000 cu. ft. Change the filter once every 4 months and enjoy clean air.

COST:

£150 for model 100, including delivery, replacement filter pack £15.00 each including postage and packaging. Running cost the same as a light bulb.

TAKE CLEAN AIR SERIOUSLY

(AIRSTREAM BY ANDA)

---

38   AIRSTREAM is a machine for
  A   cleaning walls and ceilings.
  B   bringing in fresh air from outside.
  C   removing dust from the air.
  D   warming the room.

39   When you have installed AIRSTREAM, you
  A   must keep your windows closed.
  B   will not need to clean your room.
  C   will have to change the filter regularly.
  D   must have it serviced every four months.

40   When you buy your AIRSTREAM, what else will you have to pay for?
  A   light bulbs and delivery
  B   new filters and electricity
  C   new filters and light bulbs
  D   electricity and delivery

PAPER 2   COMPOSITION   (1½ hours)

Write **two only** *of the following composition exercises. Your answers must follow exactly the instructions given and must be of between 120 and 180 words each.*

1   While your next-door neighbours are away on holiday, someone has broken into their house and stolen various things. Write a letter to your neighbours explaining what has happened and advising them what to do.

2   You are guide to a group of people on a holiday trip. Write the words you say to them about the scenery and customs in the area you are visiting.

3   'Don't do it!' I said. Write a story which begins or ends with these words.

4   What do you think the advantages and disadvantages of living in another country may be?

5   Based on your reading of **one** of these books, write on one of the following.

DONN BYRNE: *Mahatma Gandhi – The man and his message*
Give some examples of how Gandhi showed that he wanted people to change their ideas about the Untouchables.

L. P. HARTLEY: *The Go-Between*
Describe the part played in Leo's life by Jenkins and Strode.

R. L. STEVENSON: *Dr Jekyll and Mr Hyde*
Describe what kind of person Mr Utterson was and his role in the story.

PAPER 3   USE OF ENGLISH   (2 hours)

1 *Fill each of the numbered blanks in the following passage. Use only* **one** *word in each space.*

Last Tuesday I took my two nieces, aged three and five, to town in the car. It began to pour .... (1) rain so I decided I would leave the children in the car, ... (2) I dashed into a shop. I warned the girls .... (3) to touch anything and told them I would be .... (4) within a few minutes. Then I locked all the doors and left .... (5) happily looking out of the window.

   I was back at the car in .... (6) than five minutes but the girls had vanished! I could hardly .... (7) my eyes. The car doors were still locked, the .... (8) tightly shut and on the back seat were .... (9) two jackets. In a panic I ran .... (10) the corner of the street .... (11) there was no sign of them. I rushed up to a couple of passers-by and .... (12) in vain whether they had seen two small girls. Feeling quite sick .... (13) fear, I sat .... (14) the driver's seat, ... (15) to stop trembling. Suddenly, behind me I .... (16) a tapping noise and laughter. I .... (17) out of the car, ran round to open the boot and there inside .... (18) two very red-faced and excited children. They had apparently pulled out the back seat, crawled behind .... (19) and then been unable to push the seat forward again. I .... (20) wept with relief!

2 *Finish each of the following sentences in such a way that it means the same as the sentence printed before it.*

EXAMPLE: I haven't enjoyed myself so much for years.

ANSWER: It's years *since I enjoyed myself so much.*

a) Joan eats very little so as not to put on weight.

Joan eats very little because ....

b) On arrival at the shop, the goods are inspected carefully.

When the goods ....

c) Laurence hasn't seen his sister since she left for Japan.

Laurence last ....

d) Peter said he wasn't feeling well.

Peter said, 'I ....

e) John is fat because he eats so many chips.

If ....

f) 'You should take more exercise, Mr Roberts,' the doctor said, 'if you want to lose weight.'

The doctor advised ....

g) Collecting dolls from foreign countries is one of Jane's interests.

Jane is ....

h) George is not nearly as energetic as he used to be.

George used ....

i) If Joe doesn't change his ways, he will end up in prison.

Unless ....

3 *Fill the gaps in the following sentences, which are all connected with* **restaurants**.

EXAMPLE: The *waiter* asked them if they were ready to order.

a) Gino's is a very popular restaurant, so we'd better .... a table in advance if we want to eat there.

b) They couldn't decide what to eat because the .... was written in Italian.

c) They were so full that all they wanted for .... was ice-cream.

d) They were charged an inclusive price for a three-............................. meal and coffee.

e) The waiter had been very helpful so they left him a generous

   ....

4 *Complete the following sentences with a suitable expression formed from* **give**.

   EXAMPLE: They *gave out* the fact-sheets at the beginning of the meeting.

   a) At a junction, traffic on the minor road must .... to traffic on the main road.

   b) The teacher asked the students to .... their homework on Friday.

   c) They had to .... the search because it was getting dark.

   d) Can you .... me .... the record I lent you last month?

   e) My bike is so rusty I can't possibly sell it; I'll have to .... it ....

5 *Mark Barlow has applied for a job in a bank in London. He's being interviewed by the Manager, Mr Hall. Complete the numbered gaps in the following dialogue.*

   Mr Hall: Do come in and sit down, Mr Barlow.

   Mark: Thank you.

   Mr Hall: Now let's see. So you've just finished college. What (1) ....
   .... ?

   Mark: Computing, Business Studies and Economics. We had to choose three special subjects as well as doing a general course.

   Mr Hall: And why (2) .... ?

   Mark: Well, I've always wanted to work in a bank and I thought these would be the best subjects to do.

   Mr Hall: And can you (3) .... ?

   Mark: Well, I'm quite good at Spanish.

   Mr Hall: Really? Where (4) .... ?

13

Mark:	At school. We had an excellent teacher. And I know a bit of Japanese too.
Mr Hall:	That's interesting. Have (5) ....?
Mark:	No. I'd love to go there but it's a long way from England! But my parents had a Japanese lodger for six months and she taught me. It was very difficult but I learned quite a lot.
Mr Hall:	Good, good. What (6) ....?
Mark:	I'm in the local drama group and I'm keen on sport.
Mr Hall:	Most interesting. Well, that's all for the moment, Mr Barlow. Could you please wait in my secretary's office for a few minutes?
Mark:	Yes, of course. Thank you.

6 *Basing your answer on the information given below, write what you think Woodgreen Secondary School should do with the money mentioned in the newspaper article, and what would **not** be a good idea. Write in the spaces provided on pages 15 and 16, giving reasons for your opinions.* **(You do not need to use all the information.)**

£50,000 gift to inner-city school

Woodgreen Secondary School has been given £50,000 by the famous boxing champion Steve Miles, an ex-pupil.

The school was founded in 1950 and has 520 boys and 476 girls (aged 11–18). Situated in the middle of the city, it is often criticised for being old-fashioned and over-crowded.

Extract from the Head's end-of-term speech:

'. . . and despite one or two fine individual performances, I must confess to a feeling of disappointment in our academic record this year. The examination pass rate is down to 56% (compared with 72% five years ago) and only 16 pupils have obtained places at universities (five in Science subjects). On the sports field, we have failed to win . . . .'

Comments recently heard at school:

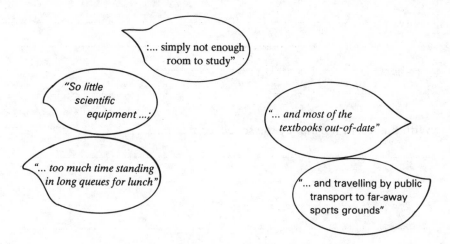

Suggestions made at the School Committee Meeting:
Each of these would cost about **£50,000**:

1.   Large sports hall facilities for basket-ball, table-tennis, gymnastics.
2.   Indoor heated swimming-pool.
3.   New computers.
4.   Laboratory extension for younger pupils (Chemistry and Physics).
5.   Private study-centre for older pupils.

Each of these would cost about **£25,000**:

1.   Two school mini-buses.
2.   Library books, tapes and videos for language courses.
3.   Coffee, cold drinks and sandwich machines.
4.   Musical instruments.
5.   A developed garden-area for relaxation.
6.   £500 annual prize (for 50 years) for the pupil who does best in work or sport each year.

(*a*) If the school spends all the money on one thing, I think they should ....

....

....

....

....

15

(b) However, it might also be a good idea to buy two things with the money. In this case I would spend £25,000 on .... because ....

....

....

....

....

With the rest of the money the school could ....

....

....

....

....

(c) I would **not** spend the money on ....

....

....

....

PAPER 4   LISTENING COMPREHENSION
(about 30 minutes)

PART ONE

You will hear a woman asking for details about life insurance. Fill in the missing information in the spaces numbered 1 to 9 on the Personal Statement below.

GOLDEN LIFE ASSURANCE PLC

PERSONAL STATEMENT

Full name *Miss Elizabeth*

> 1

Place of birth *Birmingham*

Date of birth

17 | 2 | *60*

Occupation

> 3

Present address
3 Johnstone Street,
St Pauls, Bristol

Postcode ╱

Tel. *22041*

Height *1·63m*   Weight *58 kg*

When and why did you last consult a doctor?

> 4

— for appendix operation

Are you on a diet, treatment or taking any pills or drugs?

> 5

How much do you smoke?

> 6

How much do you drink? *a few glasses of*

> 7

weekly

Do you intend to journey abroad frequently?

> 8

Do you take part in any dangerous sports?   *Yes*

If 'yes' give details

> 9

Signature   Date
Elizabeth Brown   11/6/85

PART TWO

You will now hear a radio programme about building water tanks in Botswana. For each of the questions 10 to 13 you will see four pictures. Tick one of the boxes A, B, C or D to show which picture gives the best answer to each question.

Question 10. What does the water tank look like?

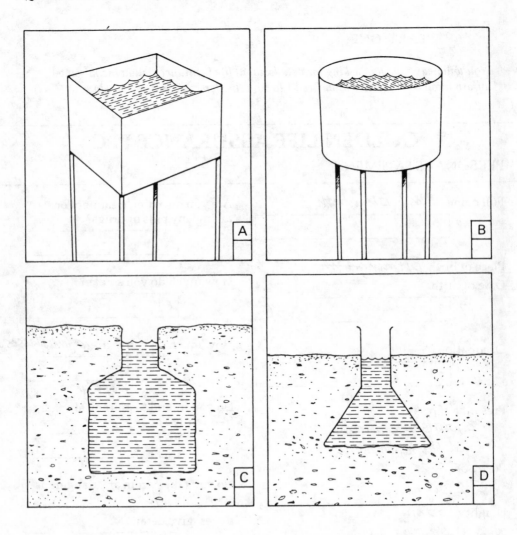

Question 11. How do they get the water out of the tank?

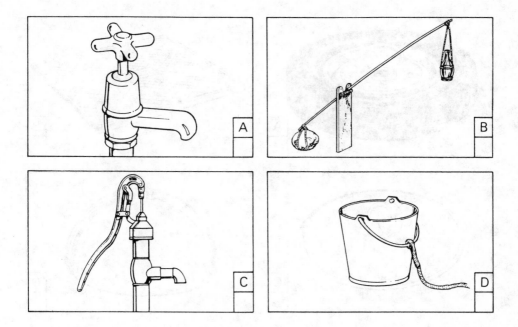

Question 12. What does the lid of the water tank look like?

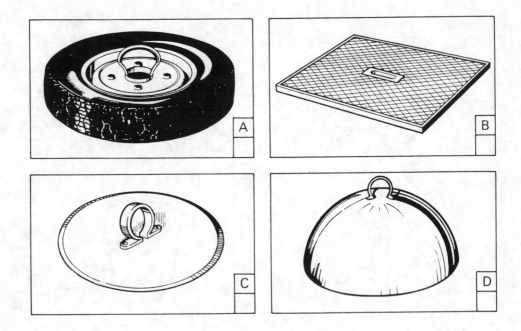

Question 13. *According to the radio programme, how do the men build the water tank?*

PART THREE

You will hear some station announcements about train departures from Birmingham station. Look at the departure board below and fill in the missing information in the spaces numbered 14 to 18.

DEPARTURES			
TIME	DESTINATION	PLATFORM	DELAYED DUE TO
11.35	Wolverhampton	14	
11.38	Taunton	15	
16	Glasgow and Edinburgh	9	damage to overhead cables
11.45	Derby	3	awaiting 17
11.52	18	4	

PART FOUR

You will hear an interview with someone called Michaela, who helps to run a club for young people. For questions 19 to 28 below, tick the boxes to show which activities organised at the Community Centre are mentioned by Michaela. If the activity is not mentioned, leave the box blank.

19	dance	
20	swimming	
21	boxing	
22	football	
23	weight training	
24	volleyball	
25	karate & kung fu	
26	brass band	
27	drama	
28	table-tennis	

PAPER 5 INTERVIEW (about 15 minutes)

You will be asked to take part in a theme-directed conversation with the examiner. You may be by yourself, with another candidate or with two other candidates. (Two examiners are present when there are three candidates.) The conversation will be based on one particular topic area, for example holidays, work, food.

A typical interview is described below.

* You will be shown one, two or three photographs and invited to talk about them.

* The examiner will then show you one or more passages and invite you to link them to the theme. You may be asked to talk a little about the content of the passage. You will *not*, however, be asked to read the passage aloud but you may quote parts of it to make your point.

* You will then be asked to take part in a communicative activity with the other candidates present and/or the examiner (or examiners). This could involve role-play, problem solving, planning, rank ordering etc. or it could be a discussion on another aspect of the general theme of the conversation. Advertisements, diagrams and other realia are often used as stimuli here.

You will find six sample First Certificate interviews at the back of this book. Your teacher can help you to prepare for this part of the examination by assuming the role of the examiner and telling you which item in the Interview Exercises you should look at.

Practice Test 2

PAPER 1   READING COMPREHENSION   (1 hour)

Answer all questions. Indicate your choice of answer in every case **on the separate answer sheet** *already given out, which should show your name and examination index number. Follow carefully the instructions about how to record your answers. Give* **one answer only** *to each question. Marks will not be deducted for wrong answers: your total score on this test will be the number of correct answers you give.*

SECTION A

In this section you must choose the word or phrase which best completes each sentence. **On your answer sheet** *indicate the letter A, B, C or D against the number of each item 1 to 25 for the word or phrase you choose.*

1 The losing team were disappointed at the result, but all the players agreed
that it had been a good ....
A play   B score   C game   D sport

2 The students were slow to catch ...., but gradually they began to
understand.
A in   B on   C away   D out

3 The soldier was punished for .... to obey his commanding officer's
orders.
A refusing   B regretting   C objecting   D resisting

4 She'll be a millionaire by the time she .... forty.
A is   B was   C will be   D is going to be

5 Some of the passengers spoke to reporters about their .... in the
burning plane.
A occasion   B happening   C event   D experience

6 .... the rise in unemployment, people still seem to be spending more.
A Nevertheless   B Meanwhile   C Despite   D Although

7 Their flat is decorated in a .... combination of colours.
A tasteful   B sweet   C delicious   D tasty

24

8 I wish you .... stop interrupting me whenever I speak.
   A will   B would   C did   D might

9 This ring is only made of plastic so it's quite ....
   A valuable   B invaluable   C worthless   D priceless

10 You can't enter this camp without .... from the General.
   A a control   B a demand   C a permit   D an allowance

11 Tony's boss doesn't want him to .... a habit of using the office phone for personal calls.
   A make   B do   C have   D increase

12 She .... her husband's job for his ill health.
   A accused   B blamed   C caused   D claimed

13 He .... the bowl of soup all over the table-cloth.
   A stained   B spilt   C scattered   D set

14 It's time we .... this old car and bought a new one.
   A will sell   B had sold   C have sold   D sold

15 As .... as I know, we have not received a bill for the new computer.
   A much   B long   C soon   D far

16 The project was rejected because of .... funds.
   A unavailable   B inconsiderable   C incomplete   D insufficient

17 She is .... to leave as soon as possible.
   A cautious   B anxious   C worried   D nervous

18 Ann agreed to stay behind; she was used to .... late.
   A working   B have worked   C work   D being worked

19 We looked everywhere but the intruder was nowhere ....
   A to see   B seen   C to be seen   D having seen

20 I haven't time to speak to him now, you'll have to put him ....
   A off   B back   C aside   D away

21 Nobody seems to be .... control of those children.
   A under   B over   C with   D in

22 The coins are .... to be over a thousand years old.
   A described   B said   C told   D mentioned

23 The traffic in town was very .... and I arrived home earlier than
   expected.
   A light   B weak   C little   D few

24 I bought this grammar book .... I could go over all the things we have
   studied this year.
   A that   B so that   C seeing that   D so far as

25 You know I'll always stand .... you if you are in trouble.
   A by   B with   C for   D up

SECTION B

*In this section you will find after each of the passages a number of questions or
unfinished statements about the passage, each with four suggested answers or ways of
finishing. You must choose the one which you think fits best according to the passage.*
On your answer sheet *indicate the letter A, B, C or D against the number of each
item 26–40 for the answer you choose. Give* **one answer only** *to each question. Read
each passage right through before choosing your answers.*

FIRST PASSAGE

A linguist is always listening, never off-duty. I invited a group of friends round
to my house, telling them that I was going to record their speech. I said I was
interested in their regional accents, and that it would take only a few minutes.
Thus, on one evening, three people turned up at my house and were shown into
my front room. When they saw the room they were a bit alarmed, for it was laid
out as a studio. In front of each easy chair there was a microphone at head
height, with wires leading to a tape-recorder in the middle of the floor. They sat
down, rather nervously, and I explained that all I wanted was for them to count
from one to twenty. Then we could relax and have a drink.

I turned on the tape-recorder and each in turn solemnly counted from one to
twenty in their best accents. When it was over, I turned the tape-recorder off
and brought round the drinks. I was sternly criticised for having such an idiotic
job and for the rest of the evening there was general jolly conversation – spoilt
only by the fact that I had to take a telephone call in another room, which
unfortunately lasted some time.

Or at least that is how it would appear. For, of course, the microphones were
not connected to the tape-recorder in the middle of the room at all but to
another one which was turning happily away in the kitchen. The participants,
having seen the visible tape-recorder turned off, paid no more attention to the
microphones which stayed in front of their chairs, only a few inches from their
mouths, thus giving excellent sound quality. And my lengthy absence meant

that I was able to obtain as natural a piece of conversation as it would be possible to find.

I should add, perhaps, that I did tell my friends what had happened to them, after the event was over, and gave them the option of destroying the tape. None of them wanted to – though for some years afterwards I was left in no doubt that I was morally obliged to them, in the sense that it always seemed to be my round when it came to the buying of drinks. Linguistic research can be a very expensive business.

26 Why did the writer ask his friends to count from one to twenty?
 A   He wanted to record how they pronounced numbers.
 B   He had to check that his tape-recorder was working.
 C   He wanted them to think that was all he wanted to record.
 D   He wanted to discover who had the best pronunciation.

27 Why did the writer leave the room in the middle of the evening?
 A   He had to make a phone call.
 B   The phone rang in another room.
 C   He wanted the others to have a conversation without him.
 D   He didn't like being criticised.

28 Which of the following words describes the recording which the writer was able to make?
 A   natural
 B   controlled
 C   prepared
 D   indistinct

29 How did his friends react when he told them what he had done?
 A   They wanted him to destroy the recordings he had made.
 B   They didn't mind at all.
 C   They were upset because they felt he had cheated them.
 D   They made him buy them drinks.

30 How did the writer record the general conversation?
 A   on the tape-recorder in the middle of the floor
 B   through hidden microphones
 C   on a tape-recorder in another room
 D   in a studio

SECOND PASSAGE

The contract was finally signed and we moved one Saturday in June. A carpenter cut the table, which had been originally constructed in a classroom, in two, and took the bookcase apart. We lowered chairs on the end of a rope down

through a window into the street below and took down the bull-fighting poster
– only to find that Raphael, who had decorated the wall, had been conscientious
enough with our money not to paint underneath. As we carried crates of books
down the sixty-seven steps, I remembered our struggles up the stairs two years
earlier.

Soon the flat was empty, with even the carpet ripped up. We stood for a
moment in the deserted waiting room and then clattered finally down the steps.

At our new address in Shaftesbury Avenue, regulations made things difficult
for the lorry which was now loaded with chairs and tables. Our driver
eventually parked in a side street and we pulled the furniture up past a large
shop-window. Saturday afternoon crowds were in the streets and we had to be
careful or chairs and tables would have gone crashing down on their heads. As
we were working a young man I had never seen before, approached us and
offered to help. He staggered up the stairs with armfuls of books, and helped me
carry up the heavy red reception desk. When we had finished, I offered to pay
him but he refused adamantly and vanished into the crowd again like some
visiting angel.

Until we got used to it, it seemed incredible that, with our resources, we were
now installed right in the centre of London. It made us feel like adventurers. In
the evening we sat in the sitting-room and there was no need to put on the
lights. Opposite were the Apollo and Globe theatres; outside the lights and
noise of traffic. A man with a concertina was singing below us. There were
shouts and then the sound of feet running down the street. In the middle of so
much life, it was like being on an island, hidden yet seeing, sheltered against
the flood.

31   The first paragraph suggests the writer worked in
    A   a bookshop.
    B   a school.
    C   a doctor's surgery.
    D   a theatre.

32   Why did they need a carpenter when they moved?
    A   Boxes had to be made for all their books.
    B   The furniture needed to be taken out through the windows.
    C   The broken furniture had to be repaired.
    D   Some of their furniture was too large to move as it was.

33   What made the move particularly difficult?
    A   The lorry was not allowed to park in the most convenient place.
    B   The lorry was very full.
    C   The lorry crashed into a shop window.
    D   It was difficult to find their new address.

34   Why does the writer call the young man an angel?
    A   He was a friend who helped them enormously in the move.
    B   It was difficult to persuade him to accept payment for his help.
    C   He disappeared after helping them.
    D   The writer didn't know who he was.

35   Why does the writer describe their new place as like being on an island?
    A   The theatres opposite were like lighthouses.
    B   They felt completely separated from the people and traffic
        surrounding them.
    C   Being in the very heart of London made the writer feel like an
        explorer.
    D   They were protected from the rain all round them.

THIRD PASSAGE

Membership

Proof of identity, showing name and present address, will be required before a Membership Card can be issued. You will receive only one Library Membership Card. It is important that you keep the card in your possession and always have it with you when you wish to borrow or renew books.

Take care of your Library Membership Card — if it is used by someone else you will be responsible for any books borrowed on it. There will be a charge for any lost books.

Please tell the librarian if you change your address, so that a new card may be given to you. A charge will be made for the replacement of lost cards.

Borrowing Books

Your Membership Card must be produced each time you wish to borrow books from the library. It will be returned to you immediately it has been read as these cards are not held in the library.

You may borrow up to 4 books. Borrowing will be made quicker and easier for everyone if the books you are taking out are given to the assistant open at the date label, with your Membership Card on the top book.

Returned books should also be presented in this way except that the Membership Card need not be shown.

Books should be returned to the library on or before the date shown on the date label. Fines will be charged on books returned late.

Renewing Books

Books may be renewed by bringing them to the library, together with your Membership Card, or by stating for each book the number on the label, the date due and your name and address. Books without the bar code will instead have a date card; please state the number on this for renewal.

P.T.O.

Books may be renewed by post, or personal visit with the details, ONCE ONLY from the initial return date. Postal renewal cards are available at all public desks in the library. Books in demand by other readers will not be renewed. Fines will be charged at the current rate on all books renewed late.

Children's Library

The same applies to books borrowed from the Children's Library. Books borrowed from the Children's Library must be taken out from the 'Books Out' desk and returned to the 'Books In' desk, both in the adult library.

REMEMBER — the staff are here to help you; please ask us if there is anything you would like to know.

PLEASE . . . DO NOT FOLD, WRITE ON OR LOSE YOUR MEMBERSHIP CARD!

36 A Library Membership Card
    A   is kept by the Library while you borrow books.
    B   need not be shown when borrowing books.
    C   can be used to borrow up to four books.
    D   carries your photograph for easy identification.

37 If another person uses your card to borrow books you will
    A   have to pay an extra charge.
    B   not be permitted to use the Library again.
    C   have to pay for any books lost by that person.
    D   be given a replacement card.

38 When returning books, you will save time if you
    A   give the number of the book.
    B   present the books so that details can be seen by the assistant.
    C   give the assistant your card before choosing any books.
    D   return your books on the date shown on the label.

39 To keep a library book for longer than the initial return date
    A   you must pay an additional charge.
    B   you have to bring the book back to the library.
    C   you can renew the book by telephone giving date and number.
    D   you may send a postal renewal card.

40 To take out children's books
    A   you follow the same procedures as for adult books.
    B   you must be below the age of 18.
    C   you should ask at the desk in the Children's Library.
    D   you need to apply for a special membership card.

PAPER 2   COMPOSITION   (1½ hours)

*Write **two only** of the following composition exercises. Your answers must follow exactly the instructions given and must be of between 120 and 180 words each.*

1   You have heard from a friend that your brother, who will be seventeen next month, is behaving foolishly and upsetting your parents. Write a letter to him for his birthday but at the same time try to persuade him to mend his ways.

2   Your neighbours are exchanging houses for a month with a family from another country, and have asked you to welcome the family and give them some useful information. Write what you say.

3   A little girl was lost and asked for your help. Describe what you did and how you found her family.

4   Describe some of the things people should do to stay fit and healthy.

5   Based on your reading of **one** of these books, write on one of the following.

Zero Hour (Cambridge University Press)
Describe **one or more** of these stories which give a particularly bitter picture of marriage.

DONN BYRNE: *Mahatma Gandhi – The man and his message*
'My life is my message.' What was Gandhi's message and how did his life illustrate it?

L. P. HARTLEY: *The Go-Between*
How far do you consider Marian's affection for Leo was genuine? Support your opinion with examples from the text.

PAPER 3 USE OF ENGLISH (2 hours)

1 *Fill each of the numbered blanks in the following passage. Use only* **one** *word in each space.*

He was born in a very poor part of London. His father ....(1) a comedian and his mother worked ....(2) a dancer and singer. ....(3) of them was very successful, however, and the family had very ....(4) money; at one time they were ....(5) poor that he and his brothers had only one pair of shoes ....(6) them and they had to take turns wearing them. The first time he himself earned any money, ...(7) dancing and singing, he was only five years old. He did many kinds of jobs, but what he loved ....(8) was working in the theatre.

........................(9) he was about 15 he joined a travelling theatre company and went on trips to America. On ....(10) such tour he was offered a part in a film, so he went to Hollywood, ...(11) he eventually became both an actor and a film director. He was known to be a perfectionist, and sometimes ....(12) the other actors repeat a scene many times ....(13) he was finally satisfied with it.

Many people found ....(14) difficult and some accused him of ....(15) mean, but it was really his early experiences of poverty ....(16) made him careful with his ....(17).

He died in Switzerland in 1977, ...(18) the age of 88. ....(19) is now a statue of him in Leicester Square, London, the city of his ....(20) and early upbringing. His name was Charlie Chaplin.

2 *Finish each of the following sentences in such a way that it means exactly the same as the sentence printed before it.*

EXAMPLE: I haven't enjoyed myself so much for years.

ANSWER: It's years *since I enjoyed myself so much.*

a) 'Will I ever find a job?' Tim said to himself.

Tim wondered ....

b) You should take a map because you might get lost in those mountains.

In case ....

c) Temperature is measured by a thermometer.

A thermometer is ....

d) You remembered to post the letter, didn't you?

You didn't ....

e) Mr Dryden mended the washing machine for me.

I had ....

f) Pat is the tallest girl in her class.

No one ....

g) To get the 40% discount, you must buy all twelve books at the same time.

You can only ....

h) 'I'm sorry I gave you the wrong number,' said Paul to Susan.

Paul apologised ....

i) Samuel started keeping a diary five years ago.

Samuel has ....

j) Please don't smoke in the kitchen.

I'd rather ....

3 *Complete the following sentences with a phrase formed with* **out of** ....

   EXAMPLE: After running twenty kilometres he was ....

   ANSWER: After running twenty kilometres he was *out of breath.*

   a) Keep this plant in the house. It won't survive ....

   b) Steve has been .... for two years and doesn't think he
      will ever find a job.

   c) They watched the ship until it was ....

   d) They had to use the stairs because the lift was ....

   e) This information is .... Haven't you got the latest
      figures?

4 *Complete the following sentences with* **one** *word related to the world of work.*

   EXAMPLE: Edward found a good .... in an office close to his home.

   ANSWER: Edward found a good *job* in an office close to his home.

   a) A .... has arisen for a new Director of Studies at the language school.

   b) He got the .... because he was always late for work.

   c) Applications are invited for the .... of secretary to the Director.

   d) The new car factory is expanding and expects to .... a thousand more
      local people.

   e) Mary wanted to work for that particular organisation because there were
      good chances of .... to a senior level.

5 *Make all the changes and additions necessary to produce, from the following sets of
   words and phrases, sentences which together make a complete letter. Note carefully
   from the example what kind of alterations need to be made. Write each sentence in
   the space provided.*

   EXAMPLE: I be very surprised / receive / letter / you this morning.

   ANSWER: *I was very surprised to receive a letter from you this
         morning.*

1 Poachers Walk
Cambridge

5 May 1988

The Manager
Royal Hotel
Kings Road
TORQUAY
TO5 7KM

Dear Sir/Madam

I stay / your hotel / 24 April / 30 April / room 415.

a) ....

On arrive / home, I realise / I leave / book / room.

b) ....

I wonder / it be find / hand in.

c) ....

It be / small, hardback book / blue cover call 'Gallions Reach' /
H.M. Tomlinson.

d) ....

I be very anxious / get / book back because it be now out / print /
it be difficult / find / bookshops.

e) ....

Also, / book be give / me / author, / signature be / front cover.

f) ....

I enclose / cheque / £1.50 / cover / cost / post it back / me.

g) ....

If, unfortunately, you not find / book, please return / cheque.

h) ....

I look forward to hearing from you soon.
Yours faithfully

Peter Hackett

6 *In the town of Mudleigh, the Council has to make a decision about what to do with a large empty field. At a recent meeting, five suggestions were made. Look at each of these, together with the other information given below, and then write two paragraphs. In your first paragraph, say which plan* **you** *think would be best and why. In the second paragraph, say which plan you think should definitely* **not** *be chosen, giving your reasons for your decision.*

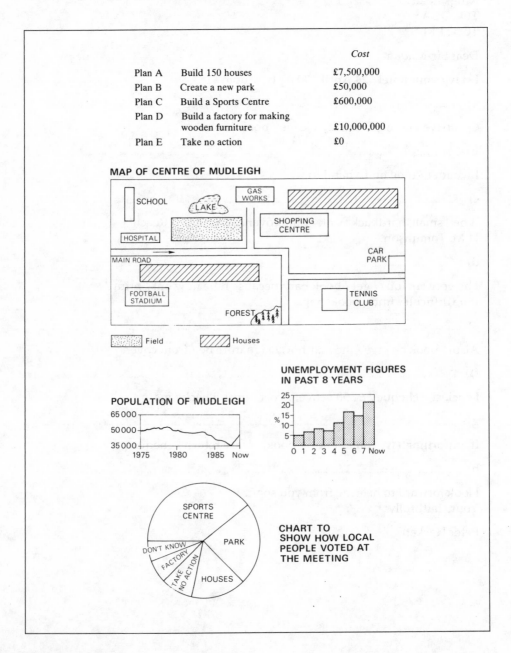

		Cost
Plan A	Build 150 houses	£7,500,000
Plan B	Create a new park	£50,000
Plan C	Build a Sports Centre	£600,000
Plan D	Build a factory for making wooden furniture	£10,000,000
Plan E	Take no action	£0

MAP OF CENTRE OF MUDLEIGH

SCHOOL LAKE GAS WORKS
HOSPITAL SHOPPING CENTRE CAR PARK
MAIN ROAD
FOOTBALL STADIUM TENNIS CLUB
FOREST

Field   Houses

POPULATION OF MUDLEIGH
65 000
50 000
35 000
1975 1980 1985 Now

UNEMPLOYMENT FIGURES IN PAST 8 YEARS
25
20
15
% 10
5
0 1 2 3 4 5 6 7 Now

SPORTS CENTRE
PARK
DON'T KNOW
FACTORY
TAKE NO ACTION
HOUSES

CHART TO SHOW HOW LOCAL PEOPLE VOTED AT THE MEETING

First paragraph

....

....

....

....

....

....

....

....

....

....

Second paragraph

....

....

....

....

....

....

....

....

....

....

PAPER 4 LISTENING COMPREHENSION
(about 30 minutes)

PART ONE

You will hear part of a radio programme in which listeners are asked to help the police with a crime at Wellington Mews. For each of the questions 1 to 5, tick one of the boxes to show the correct answer.

Question 1. Tick (√) one of the boxes to show the date of the crime.

Question 2. What does the first item stolen look like? (Tick one of the boxes.)

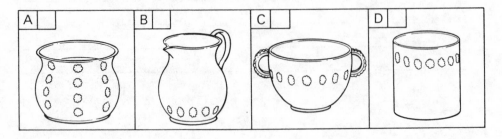

Question 3. What does the second item stolen look like? (Tick one of the boxes.)

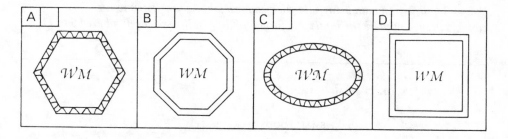

Question 4. What does the thief look like? (Tick one of the boxes.)

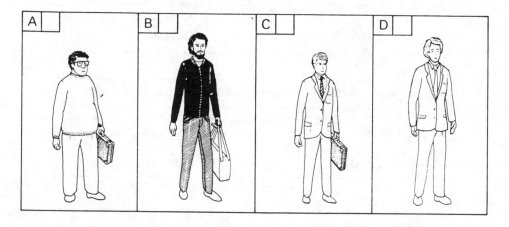

Question 5. Which vehicle was used by the thief? (Tick one of the boxes.)

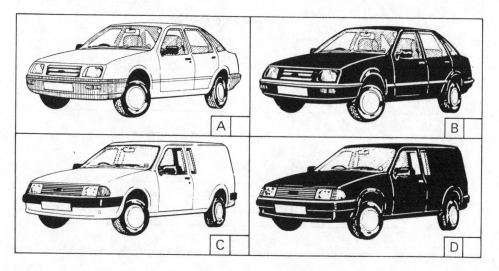

PART TWO

You will now hear a man being interviewed for a job. As you listen to the conversation, complete the interview form by filling in the spaces numbered 6 to 11.

STRICTLY CONFIDENTIAL

SMALL FOODS PACKAGING PLC

INTERVIEW FORM

INTERVIEW FOR THE POST OF   6

SURNAME (in BLOCK Capitals)	FORENAME(S)
ALLAN	Michael

EMPLOYMENT RECORD

PRESENT EMPLOYER'S NAME	POSITION HELD	LENGTH OF SERVICE
Hargreaves	Public Relations Officer	7

PREVIOUS EMPLOYMENT	POSITION HELD
	8

OTHER RELEVANT EXPERIENCE

Part-time job as   9

Experience of organising   10

FURTHER EDUCATION

EXAMINATIONS TAKEN

R.S.A. diploma in shorthand

FOREIGN LANGUAGES SPOKEN

11

PART THREE

You will hear a man trying to get people to enter a competition to win a prize. Look at the advertisement about the competition and fill in the missing information in the spaces numbered 12 to 16.

```
┌─────────────────────────────────────────────────────────────┐
│                                                               │
│        TRY YOUR LUCK AND THROW THE                            │
│                                                               │
│    DICE                        TO WIN A FANTASTIC             │
│                                                               │
│                        PRIZE!                                 │
│                                                               │
│    A BRAND NEW │12│              │ COULD BE YOURS!            │
│                                                               │
│    │13│       │ ONE TODAY FOR JUST │14│          │            │
│                                                               │
│    THROW │15│     │ SIXES ON THE DICE AND THIS FANTASTIC      │
│                                                               │
│    PRIZE WORTH │16│        │ WILL BE YOURS!!                  │
│                                                               │
└─────────────────────────────────────────────────────────────┘
```

PART FOUR

*You will hear some recorded travel information from the BBC Motoring and Travel Unit. For each of the questions 17 to 19, tick **one or more** boxes to show the correct answers. Use the map on page 42 to help you.*

17 Which motorways are affected by roadworks? (*Tick one or more.*)

☐ M1

☐ M4

☐ M5

☐ M6

18 Which services were disrupted by repair works? (*Tick one or more.*)

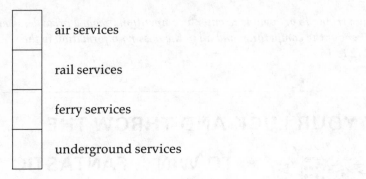

air services

rail services

ferry services

underground services

19 Which of the following statements might affect sea travellers? (*Tick one or more.*)

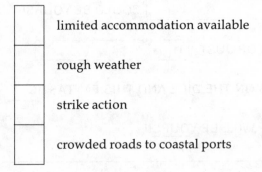

limited accommodation available

rough weather

strike action

crowded roads to coastal ports

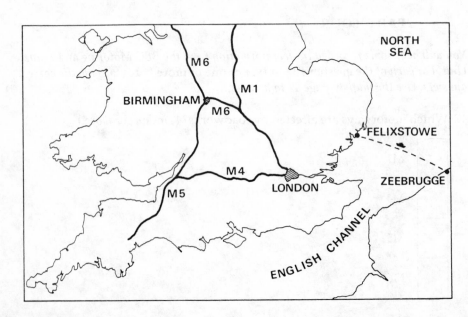

PAPER 5 INTERVIEW (about 15 minutes)

You will be asked to take part in a theme-directed conversation with the examiner. You may be by yourself, with another candidate or with two other candidates. (Two examiners are present when there are three candidates.) The conversation will be based on one particular topic area, for example holidays, work, food.

A typical interview is described below.

* You will be shown one, two or three photographs and invited to talk about them.

* The examiner will then show you one or more passages and invite you to link them to the theme. You may be asked to talk a little about the content of the passage. You will *not*, however, be asked to read the passage aloud, but you may quote parts of it to make your point.

* You will then be asked to take part in a communicative activity with the other candidates present and/or the examiner (or examiners). This could involve role-play, problem solving, planning, rank ordering etc. or it could be a discussion on another aspect of the general theme of the conversation. Advertisements, diagrams and other realia are often used as stimuli here.

You will find six sample First Certificate interviews at the back of this book. Your teacher can help you to prepare for this part of the examination by assuming the role of the examiner and telling you which item in the Interview Exercises you should look at.

Practice Test 3

PAPER 1   READING COMPREHENSION   (1 hour)

Answer all questions. Indicate your choice of answer in every case **on the separate answer sheet** *already given out, which should show your name and examination index number. Follow carefully the instructions about how to record your answers. Give* **one answer only** *to each question. Marks will not be deducted for wrong answers: your total score on this test will be the number of correct answers you give.*

SECTION A

In this section you must choose the word or phrase which best completes each sentence. **On your answer sheet** *indicate the letter A, B, C or D against the number of each item 1 to 25 for the word or phrase you choose.*

1 Let's go for a long walk, ... we?
   A will   B do   C shall   D must

2 My doctor .... me to take up swimming as it is such good exercise.
   A suggested   B proposed   C advised   D said

3 Phone me before ten; .... I'll be too busy to talk to you.
   A unless   B whether   C otherwise   D if

4 I don't .... locking the door.
   A remember   B forget   C remind   D accept

5 Fortunately the machine was not .... when it caught fire.
   A in order   B in use   C in progress   D in ruins

6 The cat was afraid when it saw its .... in the mirror.
   A picture   B look   C sight   D reflection

7 I disapprove .... people smoking in public places.
   A of   B with   C at   D on

8 They .... haven't replied to the letter we sent two months ago.
   A still   B yet   C already   D ever

9 The four-day march over the mountains was very .... for some of the soldiers.
A fierce   B hard   C lasting   D far

10 She found it hard to .... up to the fact that she would never be famous.
A come   B get   C face   D keep

11 Please leave this space .... on the enrolment form.
A absent   B blank   C missing   D undone

12 You shouldn't have criticised him in front of his friends. It was extremely .... of you.
A unfortunate   B insensitive   C insensible   D unconscious

13 He will only pass the examination if there is a(n) .... in his classwork.
A progress   B increase   C rise   D improvement

14 Come and see me when you .... your report.
A finish   B will finish   C had finished   D having finished

15 I often miss the bus because my watch is ....
A overdue   B late   C slow   D behind

16 For the first few minutes she was leading the race, then she began to fall ....
A out   B through   C back   D off

17 The passport she carried was ....
A artificial   B imitation   C untrue   D false

18 I'm tired of my neighbours .... their records at full volume every night.
A to play   B play   C having played   D playing

19 Hurry up! They've only got .... seats left.
A a little   B a few   C a lot of   D plenty of

20 Now that she is trained, she hopes to earn her living as a .... in an office.
A typewriter   B personnel   C clerk   D staff

21 .... many times I tell him, he always forgets to pass on phone messages.
A Wherever   B Whatever   C However   D Whenever

22 This sort of music was very .... in the 1940s.
A preferred   B liked   C favourite   D popular

23 They'll never .... to get here by six – the roads are quite busy today.
A manage   B arrive   C succeed   D able

24 The instructor warned the students .... sailing alone on the lake.
    A not   B from   C about   D out of

25 The children .... better leave now, it's getting late.
    A should   B had   C would   D ought

SECTION B

In this section you will find after each of the passages a number of questions or unfinished statements about the passage, each with four suggested answers or ways of finishing. You must choose the one which you think fits best according to the passage. **On your answer sheet**, *indicate the letter A, B, C or D against the number of each item 26–40 for the answer you choose. Give* **one answer only** *to each question. Read each passage right through before choosing your answers.*

FIRST PASSAGE

Charlie Stowe waited until he heard his mother snore before he got out of bed. Even then he moved with caution and tiptoed to the window. The front of the house was irregular, so that it was possible to see a light burning in his mother's room. But now all the windows were dark. . . . Charlie Stowe was frightened.

But the thought of the tobacconist's shop which his father kept down a dozen wooden stairs drew him on. He was twelve years old, and already boys at the County School laughed at him because he had never smoked a cigarette. The packets were piled twelve deep below, and the little shop lay under a thin layer of stale smoke which would completely cover up his crime. That it was a crime to steal some of his father's stock Charlie Stowe had no doubt, but he did not love his father; his father was unreal to him, a shadowy figure, pale, thin, indefinite, who noticed him only occasionally and left even punishment to his mother. For his mother he felt a strong love; . . . from her speech he judged her the friend of everyone. . . . But his father's affection and dislike were as indefinite as his movements. Tonight he had said he would be in Norwich, and yet you never knew. Charlie Stowe had no sense of safety as he crept down the wooden stairs. . . .

At the bottom of the stairs he came out quite suddenly into the little shop. It was too dark to see his way, and he did not dare touch the switch. For half a minute he sat in despair on the bottom step with his chin in his hands. Then the regular movement of the searchlight was reflected through an upper window and the boy had time to fix in memory the pile of cigarettes, the counter, and the small hole under it. The footsteps of a policeman on the pavement made him grab the first packet to his hand and dive for the hole. A light shone along the floor and a hand tried the door, then the footsteps passed on, and Charlie hid in the darkness.

At last he got his courage back by telling himself in his strangely adult way that if he were caught now there was nothing to be done about it, and he might as well have his smoke. He put a cigarette in his mouth and then remembered that he had no matches.

26   How could Charlie see that his mother's window was dark?
    A   He was standing on tiptoe.
    B   He had moved to the front of the house.
    C   He had gone downstairs to see.
    D   He could see her window from his room.

27   Charlie was frightened because
    A   he was going to steal a cigarette.
    B   the boys at school might laugh at him.
    C   he had never smoked a cigarette before.
    D   his father was waiting downstairs.

28   How did Charlie feel about his father?
    A   He liked him very much.
    B   He thought he was unpredictable.
    C   He was jealous of him.
    D   He felt safe with him.

29   As soon as he went into the shop Charlie
    A   switched the light on.
    B   felt safer.
    C   sat down on the stairs.
    D   could see the cigarettes.

30   What did Charlie do when he heard the policeman?
    A   He hid under the counter.
    B   He tried to get out of the door.
    C   He ran back upstairs.
    D   He put the cigarettes down.

31   Charlie did not smoke a cigarette because
    A   he regretted what he had done.
    B   he wanted to behave like an adult.
    C   he hadn't brought any matches.
    D   he was afraid of being caught.

SECOND PASSAGE

You would like to take good photographs of real-life situations but you have few ideas for pictures. I suggest you look around you. The everyday world is full of scenes being played by an ever-changing group of actors. You probably passed a dozen picture situations without noticing on your way to work this morning.

The realistic approach to photography has been perfected in the past by such masters as Henri Cartier-Bresson and Bill Brandt. But while you can learn a great deal from looking at the work of others, any success you can hope to achieve in this field has to come from developing an individual approach.

The main requirement for any photographer has little to do with technical matters. You must develop an awareness of the world around you and the people who inhabit it, and you should learn to notice when a situation may develop to a point where you will be able to take a good picture. Those who have reached this happy state will be prepared when that moment arises, and will simply raise their camera quickly and shoot. Others who are not so aware will be struggling with camera cases and lens caps.

Film manufacturers must be delighted at the thought of the inexperienced photographer setting out in search of the right situation and the right moment. Many miles of costly material have passed through thousands of cameras as this endless search continues. But although a lot of this waste must be put down to inexperience, you'll find that even the professionals have to use a lot of film when they are out shooting.

Not every shot is going to be a winner. If you look at the work of even the best photographers you'll notice dozens of pictures have had to be taken only because they lead up to the successful shot of a situation that the photographer has obviously been observing through the lens. You may find that you have taken one or two pictures after the right moment has passed as well. There is seldom more than one shot which stands out. There is just one point where it all comes together, and you often have to waste film to catch that precious moment.

32   How can you become a better real-life photographer?
    A   by watching other photographers at work
    B   by learning about famous photographers
    C   by just taking a great many photographs
    D   by developing skills and ideas for yourself

33   The best real-life photography depends on
    A   going out and searching for unusual situations.
    B   becoming highly skilled in camera techniques.
    C   being able to tell when a good situation might arise.
    D   having a camera which is easy and quick to use.

34   The waste of film in real-life photography is
    A   expensive and unnecessary.
    B   essential to the production of good pictures.
    C   limited to amateur photographers.
    D   the result of poor choices of subject.

35   What is likely to be most successful?
   A   taking pictures without too much preparation
   B   taking a whole series of similar pictures
   C   taking great care to set up the situation
   D   taking one picture at the right moment

36   This text is taken from
   A   a camera instruction booklet.
   B   an advertisement for film.
   C   a history of photography.
   D   an introduction to photography.

THIRD PASSAGE

EVENING COURSE

Students must apply for a place before attending any class. Applications, whether by post or in person, are dealt with strictly in the order they are received at the Adult Education Office.

You can apply:

BY POST   – use the card provided with the exact fee. You will be accepted on the course
               unless it is full, in which case we will inform you. An acknowledgement will not
               be made nor a receipt sent unless you provide a stamped addressed envelope.
               Receipts will normally be given out at the first class.

IN PERSON   – call at the Adult Education Office (ground floor, C Block) between
               approximately 9.00 am and 3.30 pm (2.30 pm on Fridays), or at the
               College Reception Desk (at the main entrance) at other times (in the
               evenings until about 7.30 pm – not Fridays).

Students should note that popular classes may be full well before the course is due to start, so that early application is strongly advised to avoid disappointment.

for the AUTUMN TERM, applications will be accepted by post (preferably) or in person from 1st August.

For the SPRING TERM, applications will be accepted from 1st December.

For the SUMMER TERM, applications will be accepted from 1st April.

---

37   Students who apply to the College by post will
    A   avoid disappointment.
    B   be sent a bill.
    C   have an advantage over people applying in person.
    D   be informed if they have not got a place.

38   What must students applying by post do?
    A   provide a stamped addressed envelope
    B   pay at the first class
    C   bring the receipt to the first class
    D   send payment with their application

39   Where can students apply in person?
    A   at the College Reception Desk after about 3.30 pm
    B   at the Adult Education Office after about 3.30 pm
    C   at the Adult Education Office at 9.30 pm
    D   at the College Reception Desk at 2.00 pm on Fridays

40   If students want to apply for the Autumn Term
    A   they should check whether the course is full.
    B   the College would rather they applied by post.
    C   applications must be received by August 1st.
    D   they must apply in person.

PAPER 2   COMPOSITION   (1½ hours)

*Write **two only** of the following composition exercises. Your answers must follow exactly the instructions given and must be of between 120 and 180 words each.*

1   You have recently seen a film which you enjoyed very much. Write a letter to a friend describing the film and explaining why he or she should go and see it.

2   It is your turn to give a short talk to a group of students in your class about a particular interest of yours. Write the talk exactly as you would give it.

3   Some friends of yours cannot decide whether to come and live in your area or go somewhere else. Give a description of your area, pointing out the advantages of living there.

4   'International sport improves international relations.' Do you agree?

5   Based on your reading of **one** of these books, write on one of the following.

DONN BYRNE: *Mahatma Gandhi – The man and his message*
Gandhi used fasting as a political weapon several times during his life.
Describe one of these fasts, the reasons for it and the effect it had.

L. P. HARTLEY: *The Go-Between*
Explain how Leo's opinion of Marian changed, and why.

R. L. STEVENSON: *Dr Jekyll and Mr Hyde*
How different is Dr Jekyll from Mr Hyde?

PAPER 3   USE OF ENGLISH   (2 hours)

1 *Fill each of the numbered blanks in the following passage. Use only* **one** *word in each space.*

Bob Geldof was born in 1953 in Dublin, where he went to school. ....(1) he was an intelligent student, he left school with few qualifications. He had ....(2) variety of jobs in England, Spain and Canada ....(3) eventually becoming a successful pop star.

However, he is now best known for the work he has done ....(4) help starving people in Ethiopia. Like many other people he ....(5) shocked by television ....(6) of people dying of hunger there in 1984. He therefore decided that he ....(7) persuade famous British pop ....(8) to make a record together, and ....(9) the profits from ....(10) to send money and food. The record, called 'Do They Know It's Christmas?' was a great success and ....(11) a lot of money, all of ....(12) was used in Ethiopia.

It soon became clear that much ....(13) money was still needed, and so in 1985 Geldof organised two huge concerts on the same day, one in England and the ....(14) in the United States. Many of the world's best known pop stars played and sang, all of them performing without ....(15) paid. The concerts were ....(16) on television throughout the world, and it has ....(17) estimated that nearly a billion people saw some ....(18) all of the broadcast. While they were ....(19) the live performance on TV, people were asked to send money and many ....(20) so. In Britain alone, over forty million pounds was given.

2 *Finish each of the following sentences in such a way that it means exactly the same as the sentence printed before it.*

EXAMPLE: I haven't enjoyed myself so much for years.

ANSWER: It's years *since I enjoyed myself so much.*

a) Sally's parents gave her a microcomputer for her birthday.

Sally ....

b) It was such bad news that Helen burst into tears.

The news ....

c) How long is it since you saw Mary?

When ....

d) If he doesn't work harder, he'll lose his job.

Unless ....

e) I'd like to visit India more than any other country in the world.

India is ....

f) Alan regretted asking Arthur to lend him £20.

Alan wished ....

g) 'When is the first day of your holiday, Peter?' Martha asked.

Martha asked Peter when ....

h) The flight to Moscow lasted three and a half hours.

It took ....

i) I work in a factory which has more than a thousand employees.

There ....

j) Belinda felt very depressed but she still went to the party.

Belinda went to the party ....

3 *Complete the following sentences with a suitable expression formed from* **get.**

EXAMPLE: My mother .... before seven o'clock most mornings.

ANSWER: My mother *gets up* before seven o'clock most mornings.

a) The thieves .... £30,000 in spite of the security guards.

b) You promised yesterday you would do the washing up this evening – you
    can't .... it now.

c) If you want to go to the Natural History Museum, take this bus and
    .... at Victoria Square.

d) I'm going away for a few days and I'll phone you as soon as I ....

e) Shirley doesn't know much Spanish but she knows enough to ....

4 *The word in capitals at the end of each of the following sentences can be used to
form a word that fits suitably in the blank space. Fill each blank in this way.*

EXAMPLES: He said 'Good morning' in a most *friendly* way.   FRIEND

My teacher *encouraged* me to take this
examination.   COURAGE

a) He cycled .... and had an accident.   CARE

b) Could you .... the picture over the sofa?   STRAIGHT

c) It's hard to buy meat on the island but fish is ....   PLENTY

d) My car is much too .... to take on a long journey.   RELY

e) In .... , I'd like to thank the many people who have
    helped me while I have been working here.   CONCLUDE

5 *Make all the changes and additions necessary to produce, from the following sets of words and phrases, sentences which together make a complete letter. Note carefully from the example what kind of alterations need to be made. Write each sentence in the space provided.*

EXAMPLE: I be very surprised / receive / letter / you this morning.

ANSWER: *I was very surprised to receive a letter from you this morning.*

47 Airport Road
Luton

2 March 1989

The Principal
The International College of Technology
Grantham
LC5 4GM

Dear Dr Smythe

Thank you / much / letter / invite me / speak / your students / careers / airline industry.

a) ....

I delight / come / answer / questions / students have.

b) ....

Generally I find it be best / start / show / video film, follow / discussion.

c) ....

Also, I have / wide selection / information leaflets which I / bring / give / any students / be interested.

d) ....

You suggest any day in / last week / March be suitable.

e) ....

I be afraid / I be / conference / Lima then.

f) ....

However, I / manage / come / 2 / 10 April.

g) ....

Please let / know which / these dates / be / convenient.

h) ....

I look forward / hear / you.

i) ....

Yours sincerely
Captain Jonathan Fitzgibbon

6 *You have been invited to organise an expedition to study the volcanic region
in the far north east of the tropical country of Bandai. Look at the map and the
advertisement below and write two paragraphs in the spaces on pages 57 and 58.
In paragraph I, explain which route you plan to take from Port Luke and what
transport you want to use. In paragraph II, explain what equipment you will need
and why.*

MAP OF BANDAI

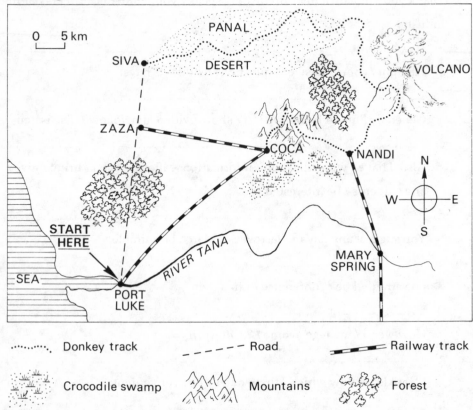

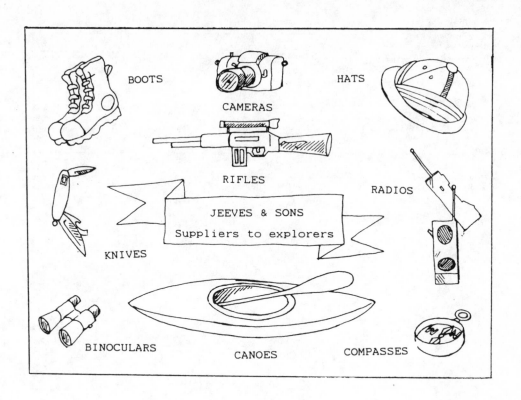

BOOTS

CAMERAS

HATS

RIFLES

RADIOS

JEEVES & SONS
Suppliers to explorers

KNIVES

BINOCULARS

CANOES

COMPASSES

I Route and Transport

....

....

....

....

....

....

....

....

....

II Equipment

....

....

....

....

....

....

....

....

....

PAPER 4   LISTENING COMPREHENSION
(about 30 minutes)

PART ONE

You will hear a conversation between two people about decorating a room. For questions 1 to 9 tick the boxes to show which items they need to get from the shop.

1 wall paper   1 ☐

2 green paint   2 ☐

3 white paint   3 ☐

4 paint brushes   4 ☐

5 brush for paste   5 ☐

6 bucket   6 ☐

7 newspaper   7 ☐

8 scissors   8 ☐

9 paste   9 ☐

PART TWO

You will hear a radio programme in which an author, Hassina Khan, talks about a book she has written. For each of the questions 10 to 13 tick one of the boxes A, B, C or D to show the correct answer.

10 What is the book about?

    A how children learn to swim

    B the problems of English families

    C a boy from an Asian family

    D a girl who feels lonely at school

A	
B	
C	
D	

11 Who wrote the book?

    A a businesswoman from Pakistan

    B the wife of an English businessman

    C a woman who was born in Pakistan

    D a woman who was born in England

A	
B	
C	
D	

12 Why did she decide to write stories?

    A She wanted to read them to the school.

    B Her talks at the school were so well-liked.

    C Children could not understand what she said.

    D Her eldest daughter asked her to do so.

A	
B	
C	
D	

13 What is a serious problem for Tariq?

    A No one plays football with him.

    B He doesn't like football.

    C Other boys make fun of him.

    D His father says he should swim.

A	
B	
C	
D	

PART THREE

You will hear someone giving details about a timetable to a group of people at a conference. For questions 14 to 23 fill in the missing information on the revised timetable in the spaces provided.

CONFERENCE: REVISED TIMETABLE

TIME	PLACE	ACTIVITY
10 a.m.	Main Hall	Coffee/Introductions
14 _____	15 _____ (Group A)	
	16 _____ (Group B)	Discussions in groups
	17 _____ (Group C)	
12.30 p.m.	18 _____	General discussion
1.00 p.m.	Main Hall	Lunch 19 _____ (if members wish)
20 _____	Lecture Theatre	21 _____
22 _____ 5.00 p.m.	Main Hall	Formal Questions 23 _____

PART FOUR

You will hear an advertisement for new houses. For each of the questions 24 to 29 tick one box to show whether the statements are true or false.

WHAT CHARTER HOMES OFFER

YOU

		True	False
24	great choice of new and old houses	24 ☐	☐
25	three and four bedrooms	25 ☐	☐
26	houses in many parts of the country	26 ☐	☐
27	special low prices now	27 ☐	☐
28	part exchange on your own home	28 ☐	☐
29	free move from your old home	29 ☐	☐

LIVE IN A STYLISH TUDOR HOME!

PAPER 5 INTERVIEW (about 15 minutes)

You will be asked to take part in a theme-directed conversation with the examiner. You may be by yourself, with another candidate or with two other candidates. (Two examiners are present when there are three candidates.) The conversation will be based on one particular topic area, for example holidays, work, food.

A typical interview is described below.

★ You will be shown one, two or three photographs and invited to talk about them.

★ The examiner will then show you one or more passages and invite you to link them to the theme. You may be asked to talk a little about the content of the passage. You will *not*, however, be asked to read the passage aloud, but you may quote parts of it to make your point.

★ You will then be asked to take part in a communicative activity with the other candidates present and/or the examiner (or examiners). This could involve role-play, problem solving, planning, rank ordering etc. or it could be a discussion on another aspect of the general theme of the conversation. Advertisements, diagrams and other realia are often used as stimuli here.

You will find six sample First Certificate interviews at the back of this book. Your teacher can help you to prepare for this part of the examination by assuming the role of the examiner and telling you which item in the Interview Exercises you should look at.

Practice Test 4

PAPER 1   READING COMPREHENSION   (1 hour)

Answer all questions. Indicate your choice of answer in every case **on the separate answer sheet** *already given out, which should show your name and examination index number. Follow carefully the instructions about how to record your answers. Give* **one answer only** *to each question. Marks will not be deducted for wrong answers: your total score on this test will be the number of correct answers you give.*

SECTION A

In this section you must choose the word or phrase which best completes each sentence. **On your answer sheet** *indicate the letter A, B, C or D against the number of each item 1 to 25 for the word or phrase you choose.*

1 They were very .... about keeping so much money in the house overnight.
   A dangerous   B willing   C nervous   D risky

2 John's father ordered .... not to stay out late again.
   A him   B to him   C that he   D for him

3 The cut on my leg is taking a long time to ....
   A heal   B right   C cure   D remedy

4 A .... is being offered for information leading to the arrest of the bank robber.
   A reward   B prize   C notice   D repayment

5 He was offered the job .... his qualifications were poor.
   A despite   B in spite of   C even though   D whereas

6 I've always .... you as my best friend.
   A regarded   B thought   C meant   D supposed

7 The job offer was too good for Jennifer to turn ....
   A off   B away   C out   D down

8 After a terrible argument with her boss, she handed in her ....
   A reservation   B reputation   C resignation   D responsibility

64

9 If you're going to Italy next week, could you please .... this present to my family?
   A fetch   B bear   C bring   D take

10 I .... to other people borrowing my books: they always forget to return them.
   A disagree   B avoid   C dislike   D object

11 Our football team lost .... three goals to nil.
   A with   B by   C to   D in

12 His laziness at work made him .... with his workmates.
   A improper   B disliked   C unpopular   D unappealing

13 I'm sure she'll do all she can ....
   A for helping   B to help   C help   D to helping

14 The company tried to make the most .... use of its limited resources.
   A financial   B cheap   C bargain   D economical

15 They didn't have .... in their suitcase for all the things they had bought on holiday.
   A room   B place   C size   D area

16 A lot needs .... to the house before anyone can move in.
   A doing   B be done   C to do   D done

17 We had so many problems with the car that .... we sold it and bought a new one.
   A at the end   B in the end   C by the end   D to the end

18 I've never been .... insulted in my life.
   A so   B such   C quite   D much

19 She had changed so much that .... anyone recognised her.
   A almost   B hardly   C not   D nearly

20 As well as .... in an office he used to have a part-time job as a waiter.
   A to work   B he worked   C he was working   D working

21 This is .... the most difficult job I've ever had to do.
   A by far   B by chance   C by heart   D by myself

22 His parents think it's time he .... married.
   A will get   B gets   C got   D would get

23 They are .... their house because they need more bedrooms.
   A increasing   B extending   C adding   D growing

24 The taxi drew .... at the gate promptly at six o'clock.
   A up   B along   C outside   D over

25 The road was .... away during the storm last night.
   A flooded   B flowed   C washed   D rained

SECTION B

In this section you will find after each of the passages a number of questions or unfinished statements about the passage, each with four suggested answers or ways of finishing. You must choose the one which you think fits best according to the passage. **On your answer sheet**, *indicate the letter A, B, C or D against the number of each item 26–40 for the answer you choose. Give* **one answer only** *to each question. Read each passage right through before choosing your answers.*

FIRST PASSAGE

Dorothea Shaw is 71 years old and nearly blind, and when she chose to live alone far away from people, she went about as far as it is possible to go to escape humanity. She lives in Belize – a country the size of Wales with a population only that of Swansea. Her home is at Gales Point, a tiny village which can be reached only by sea or air; after a 10-mile walk into the hills one finally reaches a plot of land and two small huts so hidden in the thick over-grown forest that only a handful of people know Dorothea is there.

   She lives happily and totally alone – growing her vegetables, looking after her trees and dogs, cats and chickens. Once a month or so an old friend passes by with her food supplies and mail – usually including a letter from her sister in Scunthorpe and some bits of clothing from friends in Canada. Sometimes a local man will come and chop wood for her and the occasional group of British soldiers will come across her and be greeted with the offer of a cup of coffee.

   At night she lies in her tiny sleeping hut with the dogs on the floor, the cats on the table near the typewriter and one of the hens settled down in a corner of the packed bookshelf, and listens for hours to any Spanish, English, German or French broadcasts she can find on her radio. Sometimes she gets lonely but most of the time the animals and the radio are company enough.

   But recently the very things which she had escaped from and hidden from so well have begun to catch up with her. The peace of the forest has been destroyed by the roar of earth-moving machines not many miles away. Humanity and the 20th century, once only heard of distantly on the radio, are now on her doorstep. Things began to change three years ago. The new main north-south highway in Belize was cut through the forest only four or five miles away. 'Now more and more people know I'm here,' she says. 'I feel more threatened each day.'

26   Dorothea's huts
     A   have always been her home.
     B   are entirely surrounded by trees.
     C   were built for just a few people.
     D   are in a country with the same population as Wales.

27   Dorothea lives in the forest because
     A   she is too old to move.
     B   machines destroyed her home.
     C   she has nowhere to live.
     D   she doesn't like living near people.

28   To keep her company, Dorothea has
     A   her sister.
     B   some animals.
     C   friends from Canada.
     D   a postman.

29   Dorothea spends a lot of time
     A   growing all the food she needs.
     B   chopping down trees.
     C   listening to the radio.
     D   studying languages.

30   In the last three years, Dorothea has been disturbed by
     A   the making of a new road.
     B   what she has heard on the radio.
     C   people visiting her home.
     D   threats of violence.

SECOND PASSAGE

Did you know that if you want your pet cat to live as long as possible you should choose an ordinary female cat, keep a close eye on her in spring and summer, and make sure that she is not black, or black and white? It has been discovered that male cats wander further from home, and of the large number of cats killed on the roads in spring and summer, a surprisingly high percentage are black or black and white.

Did you know, too, that domestic cats regard their owners as fellow members of the cat family and make many more sounds to us than they do to other cats when living in groups? They have worked out that we communicate by sound – and so learn a vocabulary we will understand to get their message over.

The way cats have learned to live with, and be looked after by, man, without losing their hunting and killing abilities or their mental independence, is a good reason for studying them, some scientists say.

A study of the suburban cat in Barking in Essex showed that outside the home they adopted the same hunting and exploring habits as wild cats. The female cats covered a territory limited to house and garden, while male cats travelled over an area ten times as large.

Though many people think the opposite, a cat is very practical about defending its territory. Its attitude depends on its confidence about the cat it faces, following the experience of its previous meetings. Females and young males often hide when fierce adult males turn up on their territory.

Female cats seem to feel no tension between their affectionate relationships with humans and their life 'in the wild'. It is the male cats which occasionally show signs of anxiety indicating that they are suffering from strain.

31 Why do cats make a wider range of sounds when communicating with people?
    A   They are used to doing this with other cats.
    B   They are taught to do so by their owners.
    C   They are copying human behaviour.
    D   They wish to be considered human beings.

32 Why are domestic cats of special interest to scientists?
    A   They are fierce and clever hunters.
    B   They have been domesticated for a very long time.
    C   They have lost all traces of wild behaviour.
    D   They lead both wild and domesticated lives.

33 In what ways are wild cats and domestic cats alike?
    A   They cover a wide territory.
    B   They tend to fight.
    C   They hunt and explore.
    D   They like to be alone.

34 When on their own territory cats
    A   hide from all strange cats.
    B   allow only familiar cats to cross.
    C   chase larger cats.
    D   allow fiercer cats to cross.

35 Compared with female cats, male cats tend to
    A   be mostly black or black and white.
    B   show less affection to humans.
    C   hunt more successfully.
    D   suffer more frequently from nervous strain.

THIRD PASSAGE

The Times is not an easy paper to read. It would mean little to the two million adults in Britain who cannot even read more popular papers. It would also be difficult to understand for many to whom English is a second language.

Yet even those who read *The Times* easily and with pleasure might have difficulty with official forms, leaflets and legal agreements.

Ordinary people's lives are governed by forms and notices from the moment their birth is registered until the day they die. Yet many can make no sense of the words on the bits of paper.

It is 33 years since Sir Ernest Gowers wrote a book called *Plain Words* to guide civil servants in writing clear English. Sadly, officials who are writing now do not seem to have read the book.

They excuse the fact that much of what they write cannot be understood by arguing that complicated schemes must have complicated explanations. They also claim readers would think it an insult to their intelligence to be addressed in simple English.

They think long words and fine phrases make what they have to say seem more important. They do not care very much if customers and clients remain ignorant. Public ignorance makes their job easier.

As a result we have forms that even people who can read well cannot fill in correctly. Important agreements are based on unreadable small print.

Warning notices on dangerous materials are printed so small that few people would read and understand them before an accident, let alone after it.

The legal pressure on businesses to use simpler language has made a difference, even if lawyers and courts themselves still use the language ordinary people cannot read. Companies can now make big profits from simplifying the language of contracts and complicated documents for fees of up to $10,000 for each job.

In Britain an organisation called The Plain English Movement was set up by Martin Cutts and Chrissi Maher. They started by producing a newspaper in Liverpool for adults who had difficulty in reading. Then they ran an advice centre in Salford, simplifying forms and leaflets for people claiming unemployment and sickness benefits.

The Movement has had some successes. Not least is that simplifying such leaflets to four pages with sentences averaging only 10 words has saved millions of pieces of paper a year.

36   Why is it important to simplify official language, according to the text?
    A   so that *Times* readers can understand it
    B   because it takes too long to produce the present paperwork
    C   because everyone needs to understand it
    D   to support the Plain English Movement

37 Why does the writer mention *Plain Words*?
   A   because he does not approve of the work of civil servants
   B   because he thinks today's civil servants should read it
   C   to show where the Plain English Movement took its ideas from
   D   to celebrate an important publication

38 Civil servants say they use complicated language because
   A   they do not wish to show their own ignorance.
   B   it is not part of their training to read *Plain Words*.
   C   people do not expect to understand every word of official language.
   D   the language must be difficult if the content is complex.

39 The aim of the Plain English Movement is to
   A   encourage the use of simple written English in public life.
   B   make money by simplifying contracts and complicated documents.
   C   produce a newspaper in Liverpool for adults with reading
        difficulties.
   D   run advice centres throughout Britain.

40 According to the text, one result of the Plain English Movement has
   been to
   A   simplify the language of lawyers and courts.
   B   help people to read the small print of agreements.
   C   reduce the cost of producing leaflets.
   D   help many more people get benefit payments.

PAPER 2 COMPOSITION (1½ hours)

*Write **two only** of the following composition exercises. Your answers must follow exactly the instructions given and must be of between 120 and 180 words each.*

1   You recently spent a holiday with some friends on their farm. Write to thank them and describe some of the things you enjoyed most during your stay.

2   You are asked to give a talk to a group of school children on the importance of road safety. What advice do you give them?

3   Describe a day at work or at school when everything went wrong. Explain what happened to you and how the day ended.

4   'Every family should have a computer in the home.' Do you agree?

5   Based on your reading of **one** of these books, write on one of the following.

   DONN BYRNE: *Mahatma Gandhi – The man and his message*
   'I am a politician trying my hardest to be a saint.' Do you think Gandhi was a politician or a saint?

   L. P. HARTLEY: *The Go-Between*
   Explain how Leo felt about the situation of being a 'go-between'.

   R. L. STEVENSON: *Dr Jekyll and Mr Hyde*
   'Break the door down, Poole!'
   Describe the events leading up to the discovery of Mr Hyde's body in the study. Had he taken his own life?

PAPER 3   USE OF ENGLISH   (2 hours)

1 *Fill each of the numbered blanks in the following passage. Use only **one** word in
each space.*

In 1960, Laura Ashley, a housewife with young children, began designing
and selling clothes. After some early success, ...(1) husband,
Bernard, ...(2) experienced businessman, joined her
...............(3) was able to provide considerable help and advice. The
business expanded rapidly. Laura ....(4) started working
...............(5) home, ...(6) soon there were several 'Laura Ashley'
shops where women could buy pretty, traditional clothes in a country style,
...............(7) of natural materials. ....(8) the 1980s the company
had developed ....(9) a multi-million pound international organisation with branches in places as ....(10) apart as London, Brussels,
San Francisco and Tokyo.

   Laura Ashley was a woman ....(11) simple tastes and strong moral
beliefs. She was born in Wales and one of her largest factories producing
clothes ....(12) situated in the countryside there. Her employees
were encouraged to lead healthy lives, enjoy the fresh air and a good diet.
Many of the Ashley family were involved ....(13) the business, but
in 1985 ....(14) was decided that the public ....(15) be
given the opportunity to invest money in the company. Obviously this was
...............(16) major development and a clear sign of commercial success.
But the woman ....(17) ideas had been the basis of the company's
development did not live to see it. She ....(18) down the stairs
...............(19) staying at a friend's house and died in hospital a few days
...............(20). She was only sixty-one.

2 *Finish each of the following sentences in such a way that it means the same as the sentence printed before it.*

EXAMPLE: I haven't enjoyed myself so much for years.

ANSWER: It's years *since I enjoyed myself so much.*

a) Mr Hill teaches his students to understand different English accents.

Mr Hill's students ....

b) It was such a boring film that we left before the end.

The film ....

c) Robert and Catherine have been married for four years.

It's four years ....

d) Elizabeth got a bad cough because she started smoking cigarettes.

If Elizabeth ....

e) 'Can I have a new bicycle?' said Anna to her mother.

Anna asked ....

f) Don't blame me if the tin-opener's broken.

It's not ....

g) Although he had a bad cold, William still went to work.

In spite ....

h) Barbara plays squash better than Mike.

Mike doesn't ....

i) Whose suitcase is this?

Who does ....

j) The train journey from London to Bristol takes two hours.

It is a ....

3 *Complete each sentence with a word connected with the idea of* **one**.

EXAMPLE: I've only been to Bristol .... before, and that was many years ago.

ANSWER: I've only been to Bristol *once* before, and that was many years ago.

a) I don't like being an .... child.

b) Please can I have a .... ticket to Manchester.

c) Although Aunt Harriet lived .... she had lots of friends who came to visit her.

d) This group of words is unusual because the plural is the same as the

....

e) The guide told the tourists that the museum had a .... collection of Anglo-Saxon manuscripts.

4 *Complete the following sentences with a word to do with food and drink.*

EXAMPLE: It is healthier to eat fish which has been .... rather than fried.

ANSWER: It is healthier to eat fish which has been *grilled* rather than fried.

a) I put a spoonful of sugar in Mary's tea, but she added two more to make it even ....

b) 'I'd like some really tender meat this time,' said Mrs Jones to the butcher. 'That steak you sold me last week was ....'

c) These sandwiches may not be stale but they are certainly not .... either.

d) You'll only need a little of this sauce because it has a very strong ....

e) George left the milk out of the fridge and when he went to use it he realised it was ....

5 *In the following conversation, the parts numbered 1–6 have been left out. Complete them suitably.*

Liz: Hello, Ann! You're looking very fit and well.

Ann: I've just come back from a holiday in Wales.

Liz: Oh, I wish I (1) ....

Ann: Why didn't you go anywhere this year?

Liz: Because (2) ....

Ann: But it didn't cost me much at all. I stayed at a Youth Hostel for £3 a night and it was really nice.

Liz: Aren't (3) .... ?

Ann: No, they're for people of all ages, although I suppose most of those I met were quite young.

Liz: Can (4) .... ?

Ann: Yes, but only breakfast and dinner. They are quite cheap.

Liz: What (5) .... ?

Ann: It was quite good – simple but tasty.

Liz: It sounds great. Where can (6) .... ?

Ann: Well, I've got a leaflet I could give you with some information in it.

Liz: Thanks, Ann. That would be very helpful.

6 *You are a student at a language school. The school has a social club which organises visits, parties and activities. There are also books, magazines, cassettes and videos which students can use. The teachers have asked your opinion on which of the videos illustrated below would be most useful and enjoyable for the students. Look at the details and then write your choices on page 77, giving reasons for your answers.*

Nothing prepared him for our world of change

The Last Emperor

A true story

"Born a god,
died a gardener"

HAPPY BIRTHDAY, AUSTRALIA!

From a convict settlement to a modern,
multi-racial society ......
Australia, the first 200 years.

WILD LIFE TODAY

How high do eagles fly?

Squirrels — friends or enemies?

Where do salmon breed?

Join David Attenborough for a bird's-eye view of the
wonders and beauty of nature

FAWLTY TOWERS

H O T E L

More comedy fun

at the craziest hotel in the land!

Sometimes the guests are even

funnier than

Basil, Sybil and their famous

waiter!!

H O T E L

THE FLY

Stomach-churning horror story
of a scientist's experiment which
goes wrong .... and turns him into
a grotesque human fly!

BODY LANGUAGE

A full-length keep-fit programme
with musical instructions for
each exercise ....

.....and special advice from a top gymnast!

Cooking

for

one

Delia Smith shows you how to add
variety to <u>your</u> meals.

Throne of Blood

directed by
Akira Kurosawa,
set in
medieval Japan
and based on
Shakespeare's 'Macbeth'.

With English subtitles.

A violent, exciting film.

First choice: ....

....

....

....

....

Second choice: ....

....

....

....

One video I would *not* recommend ....

....

....

....

PAPER 4   LISTENING COMPREHENSION
(about 30 minutes)

PART ONE

You will hear a court case about a road accident. For each of the questions 1–10 tick one box to show whether each statement is true or false.

		True	False
1 Martha Dobbs lives at 42 South Mansions.	1		
2 The accident happened just after Christmas.	2		
3 The pedestrian crossing is near a junction.	3		
4 It was already very dark.	4		
5 The roads were wet.	5		
6 The man started to cross without looking.	6		
7 She said the car was going too fast.	7		
8 The motorcycle hit the car.	8		
9 The pedestrian was injured in the accident.	9		
10 She wasn't sure about the number of the motorcycle.	10		

PART TWO

You will hear a conversation about birthday presents. Choose from the following list the items that best match the opinions expressed and write them down in the spaces numbered 11 to 15.

record
camera
watch
books
handbag
perfume
food
jewellery
picture
glasses

11 .... possibly, but probably not a present she will enjoy that much

12 .... likely to have them already

13 .... used this idea at Christmas

14 .... in the circumstances, not very suitable

15 .... good idea, even if they may be quite expensive

PART THREE

You will hear a woman talking about a new kind of gas cooker. For questions 16 to 25, tick the boxes to show which of the following features have been mentioned. If the feature is not mentioned, leave the box blank.

16 a glass oven door	16	
17 a fold-away grill	17	
18 a fold-away drawer	18	
19 a self-cleaning oven	19	
20 an automatic oven	20	

>>>→

21 a plate rack	21
22 four high-speed burners	22
23 an oven light	23
24 a double oven	24
25 electronic controls	25

PART FOUR

You will hear a recorded telephone announcement giving a recipe for stuffed pancakes. For each of the questions 26 and 27, tick one of the boxes A, B, C or D to show which is the correct answer. For questions 28 to 31, fill in the missing information in the spaces provided.

Question 26. Tick one of the boxes, A, B, C or D to show which quantities of cheese, butter and milk are needed for the filling of the pancakes according to the recipe.

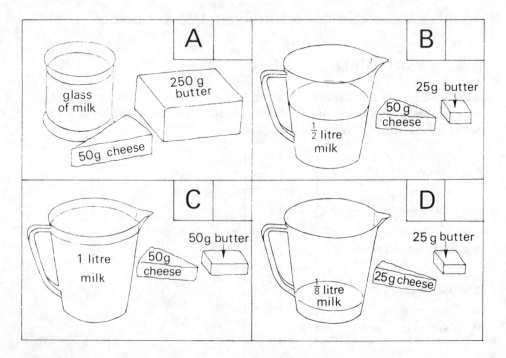

Question 27. Tick one of the boxes A, B, C or D to show which other items are needed for the recipe.

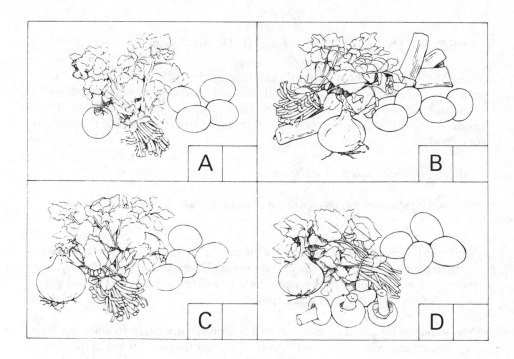

For questions 28 to 31 fill in the missing information in the spaces provided.

Now to make: cook eight | 28 _____ | and keep warm.

Fry onions in butter, stir in | 29 _____ | and cook for a further
two minutes.

Remove from heat, add | 30 _____ | and bring to the boil.

Cook for two minutes.

Add the cheese and watercress to the sauce with | 31 _____ |

Season and divide between the pancakes.

Roll them up and reheat.

PAPER 5 INTERVIEW (about 15 minutes)

You will be asked to take part in a theme-directed conversation with the examiner. You may be by yourself, with another candidate or with two other candidates. (Two examiners are present when there are three candidates.) The conversation will be based on one particular topic area, for example holidays, work, food.

A typical interview is described below.

★ You will be shown one, two or three photographs and invited to talk about them.

★ The examiner will then show you one or more passages and invite you to link them to the theme. You may be asked to talk a little about the content of the passage. You will *not*, however, be asked to read the passage aloud, but you may quote parts of it to make your point.

★ You will then be asked to take part in a communicative activity with the other candidates present and/or the examiner (or examiners). This could involve role-play, problem solving, planning, rank ordering etc. or it could be a discussion on another aspect of the general theme of the conversation. Advertisements, diagrams and other realia are often used as stimuli here.

You will find six sample First Certificate interviews at the back of this book. Your teacher can help you to prepare for this part of the examination by assuming the role of the examiner and telling you which item in the Interview Exercises you should look at.

Practice Test 5

PAPER 1   READING COMPREHENSION   (1 hour)

Answer all questions. Indicate your choice of answer in every case **on the separate answer sheet** *already given out, which should show your name and examination index number. Follow carefully the instructions about how to record your answers. Give* **one answer only** *to each question. Marks will not be deducted for wrong answers: your total score on this test will be the number of correct answers you give.*

SECTION A

In this section you must choose the word or phrase which best completes each sentence. **On your answer sheet** *indicate the letter A, B, C or D against the number of each item 1 to 25 for the word or phrase you choose.*

1 He .... me by asking me stupid questions while I am working.
   A annoys   B quarrels   C damages   D interferes

2 I am .... tired to think about that problem at the moment.
   A simply   B nearly   C far too   D much more

3 I don't remember .... the front door when I left home this morning.
   A to lock   B locking   C locked   D to have locked

4 There was no .... in waiting longer than half an hour so we left.
   A good   B point   C worth   D use

5 The child was told to eat all his vegetables or .... he would get no ice-cream.
   A in case   B else   C instead   D in fact

6 .... you have no key, you will have to get back before I go out.
   A Although   B Provided   C As   D Unless

7 The question of late payment of bills was .... again at the board meeting.
   A risen   B raised   C brought   D taken

8 .... the time you get to the theatre, the play will have finished.
   A Until   B In   C By   D On

9 Since my mother died, my closest .... is my cousin.
   A relative   B parent   C person   D related

10 James should have stayed out of the sun as his skin is so ....
   A sensible   B sensitive   C insensible   D senseless

11 Have you any objections .... this new road scheme?
   A with   B for   C at   D to

12 To get a passport, you must send in your birth .... and two photos.
   A certificate   B licence   C paper   D card

13 The job was more difficult than I .... expected it to be.
   A would   B had   C have   D might

14 She wrapped the small parcel in paper and tied it with ....
   A wire   B string   C rope   D line

15 He just couldn't open the jar .... hard he tried.
   A whatever   B however   C moreover   D even

16 Their washing-machine was out of ...., so they couldn't wash any clothes.
   A activity   B work   C order   D condition

17 Could you .... me how to use this new telephone?
   A explain   B show   C say   D remember

18 His wife's death was a terrible shock and it took him a long time to .... it.
   A get round   B come through   C go over   D get over

19 They'd like to move to New York, but their children will never agree ....
   A with going   B to go   C with go   D going

20 When she looked in her purse she found she had been ....
   A broken   B thieved   C stolen   D robbed

21 I have told him never .... here again.
   A come   B comes   C came   D to come

22 A good friend will .... you when you're having problems.
   A stand by   B stand out for   C stand against   D stand in

23 The fruit tasted sweet, rather .... a peach.
   A more   B like   C as   D similar

24 Her car's outside so I suppose she .... have arrived.
   A must   B can   C should   D ought

25 My sister is an expert on wildlife and its ....
   A conserve   B preserve   C reservation   D conservation

SECTION B

*In this section you will find after each of the passages a number of questions or
unfinished statements about the passage, each with four suggested answers or ways of
finishing. You must choose the one which you think fits best according to the passage.*
On your answer sheet, *indicate the letter A, B, C or D against the number of each
item 26–40 for the answer you choose. Give* **one answer only** *to each question. Read
each passage right through before choosing your answers.*

FIRST PASSAGE

Here in the hills were buffaloes. I had even, in my very young days – when I
could not live till I had killed one of each kind of African animal – shot a bull out
here. Later on, when I was not so keen to shoot as to watch the wild animals, I
had been out to see them again. I had camped in the hills bringing my servants,
tents and food with me but twice I had had to go back without success.

But one afternoon as I was having tea with some friends. . . . outside the
house, Denys came flying from Nairobi and went over our heads out west-
wards; a little while after he turned and came back and landed on the farm.
Lady Delamere and I drove down to the plain to fetch him up, but he would not
get out of his aeroplane.

'The buffalo are out feeding in the hills,' he said, 'come out and have a look at
them.'

'I cannot come,' I said. 'I have got a tea-party up at the house.'

'But we will go and see them and be back in a quarter of an hour,' he said.

This sounded to me like the suggestions which people make to you in a
dream. Lady Delamere would not fly so I went up with him. It did not take us
long to see the buffalo from the air; we counted them as they peacefully mixed
and separated. There was one very old big black male, one or two younger
males, and a number of young ones. The open ground on which they walked
was closed in by bushes; had a stranger approached on the ground they would
have heard or scented him at once, but they were not prepared for advance from
the air. They heard the noise of our machine and stopped feeding, but they did
not seem to have it in them to look up. In the end they realised that something
very strange was about; the old male first walked out in front of the rest.
Suddenly he began to go down the valley side and after a moment he broke into
a run. The whole group now followed him, rushing headlong down, and as they
plunged into the bushes, dust and loose stones rose behind them. In a small

wood of low trees they stopped and kept close together. Here they believed themselves to be out of sight, and so they were to anything moving along the ground, but they could not hide themselves from the eyes of the bird of the air. We flew up and away. It was like having been taken into the heart of the Ngong Hills by a secret unknown road.

When I came back to my tea-party the teapot on the stone was still so hot that I burned my fingers on it.

26   When the author was young she
    A   was keen to kill as many animals as possible.
    B   had failed to find the buffalo.
    C   was keen to shoot one of every sort of African animal.
    D   preferred watching wild animals to shooting them.

27   Lady Delamere and the author went to the aeroplane
    A   to pick Denys up and take him back to the tea-party.
    B   to talk to Denys.
    C   to persuade Denys to leave the plane.
    D   because they wanted to go up in the plane.

28   Denys said it would only take a quarter of an hour to go and see the buffalo
    A   but it took much longer than that.
    B   and he was right.
    C   if they went by a secret route.
    D   but it wasn't a serious suggestion.

29   When the buffalo heard the noise of the plane they
    A   looked up at it.
    B   ran away immediately.
    C   continued feeding.
    D   were puzzled and nervous.

30   The buffalo felt safe when they reached the wood because they
    A   thought they couldn't be seen.
    B   could only be seen from the ground.
    C   could only be seen if the plane flew higher.
    D   could not see the plane.

SECOND PASSAGE

San Francisco is where I grew up between the ages of two and ten and where I lived for a period when I was about 13 and again as a married man from the ages of 37 to 51. So quite a big slice of my life has been spent there. My mother, who is now 90, still lives in Los Gatos, about 60 miles south of San Francisco. Even though I have since lived in Switzerland and settled in London over 25 years ago, I have kept property in California for sentimental reasons.

I was born in New York and I love the United States. It is still a land of enormous drive, strength, imagination and opportunity. I know it well, having played in every town and, during the war, in every army camp. I have grown new roots in London as I did in Switzerland and if I am asked now where I want to live permanently, I would say London. But I will always remain an American citizen.

Climatically, San Francisco and London are similar and so are the people who settle in both cities. San Francisco is sophisticated, and like London, has many parks and squares. Every day my sisters and I were taken to play in the parks as children. We had an English upbringing in terms of plenty of fresh air and outdoor games. I didn't go to school. My whole formal education consisted of some three hours when I was five. I was sent to school but came home at noon on the first day and said I didn't enjoy it, hadn't learned anything and couldn't see the point of a lot of children sitting restlessly while a teacher taught from a big book. My parents decided, wisely I think, that school was not for me and I never went back.

My mother then took over my education and brought up my two sisters and me rather in the way of an educated English lady. The emphasis was on languages and reading rather than sciences and mathematics. Sometimes she taught us herself, but we also had other teachers and we were kept to a strict routine. About once a week we walked to Golden Gate Park which led down to the sea and on our walks my mother taught me to read music. One day I noticed a little windmill in the window of a shop we passed on our way to the park and I remember now how my heart yearned for it. I couldn't roll my 'r's when I was small and my mother who was a perfectionist regarding pronunciation, said if I could pronounce an 'r' well I'd have the windmill. I practised and practised and one morning woke everybody up with my 'r's. I got the windmill. I usually get the things I want in life – but I work for them and dream of them.

31   When the writer was twelve he was living in
    A   San Francisco.
    B   Los Gatos.
    C   London.
    D   a place unknown to the reader.

32   During the war, the writer
    A   became an American soldier.
    B   went camping all over the country.
    C   gave concerts for soldiers.
    D   left the United States.

33   The writer did not attend school in America because
    A   his mother wanted him to go to school in England.
    B   his parents did not think he was suited to formal education.
    C   his mother preferred him to play outdoors in the parks.
    D   he couldn't get on with the other children.

34   He was educated at home by
    A   his mother and other teachers.
    B   an educated English lady.
    C   his mother amd sisters.
    D   teachers of languages and science.

35   The writer managed to obtain the little windmill he wanted by
    A   borrowing the money for it.
    B   learning to read music.
    C   succeeding in speaking properly.
    D   working hard at his lessons.

THIRD PASSAGE

Picture a network of quiet canals spanned by tiny donkey-backed bridges and bordered by medieval houses and charming, old hanging gardens — Bruges belongs so completely to the past that you'll feel you've stepped back in time to a more peaceful, leisurely way of life.

Day One. Your holiday starts when you board our luxury coach at 10.30 am to travel to Dover for the lunchtime crossing to Calais. A drive through the countryside of northern France and Belgium brings you to Bruges in the late afternoon where you'll be checking into the Grand Hotel du Sablon, a popular hotel with restaurants, a bar and comfortable bedrooms, situated near the picturesque market place.

After dinner, the evening is yours to explore this fascinating town — just about everything is within walking distance and the odds are that you'll find yourself breaking off to stop at a local cafe for coffee or a drink!

Day Two. You'll have breakfast at the hotel and then we'll take you on a guided walking tour of the town. Bruges has kept its Middle Ages character and this is reflected in the beauty of the buildings.

The contrast between the imposing historical buildings and the fascinating network of canals is irresistible. In the afternoon we'll be taking you on a canal cruise — perhaps the best way to savour the atmosphere of Bruges. And don't forget that Bruges is justly famous for beautiful chocolates and hand-made lace. You'll find you have plenty of time to shop at leisure after the canal cruise before returning to your hotel for dinner.

Day Three. Today we have planned a full-day excursion to Ghent and Brussels. Ghent, famed for its collection of Flemish masters, is built on a great number of small islands. It's the centre of the cotton trade and the flower industry and has grown up around a fine medieval fortress.

Brussels, the capital of Belgium, is a bustling city where modern architecture complements the beauty of the old town. You'll return to your hotel in Bruges for dinner.

Day Four. After breakfast you'll have time for a last look around Bruges before the drive to Calais and the ferry crossing to Dover. You'll arrive back in London at about 6 o'clock in the evening.

Departures are on Fridays, August 8 and 29, October 10, 17 and 24 and Thursdays, September 4, 18 and 25 and October 2. Prices are from £99, based on two people sharing a twin-bedded room. We know you'll be fascinated by the beauty of Belgium and its interesting towns. And we can offer you a very special deal on rail travel to London to pick up your coach — for just £10 return (second class) you can travel to London from any station in England, Scotland or Wales. Just fill in the coupon for full details.

36 On Day One you will have
    A breakfast on board the boat.
    B lunch in the hotel.
    C dinner in northern France.
    D dinner in Belgium.

37 Day Two consists of
    A 1 organised trip.
    B 2 organised trips.
    C 3 organised trips.
    D a free day for you to explore.

38 Where will you be staying?
    A two nights in Bruges and one in Brussels
    B three nights in Bruges
    C one night each in Bruges, Brussels and Calais
    D two nights in Calais and one in Bruges

39 This holiday is for people who
    A want peace and quiet.
    B like coach tours.
    C enjoy sightseeing.
    D like sailing.

40 Departures for this trip to Bruges are on
    A certain Fridays in September.
    B certain Thursdays in August.
    C certain Fridays in August.
    D certain Fridays and Thursdays in September.

PAPER 2   COMPOSITION   (1½ hours)

*Write **two only** of the following composition exercises. Your answers must follow exactly the instructions given and must be of between 120 and 180 words each.*

1   Your car or motorbike has been stolen. Write a formal letter to an insurance company giving a description of the vehicle and the circumstances of the theft.

2   You have new neighbours who ask you about your district, in particular the transport and shopping facilities. What do you say to them?

3   Describe what could be done to prevent violence at sports events.

4   Some people think it is wrong to keep animals in zoos nowadays. Do you agree?

5   Based on your reading of **one** of these books, write on one of the following.

DONN BYRNE: *Mahatma Gandhi – The man and his message*
How did Gandhi break the Salt Law and what happened as a result of his action?

L. P. HARTLEY: *The Go-Between*
Describe life at Brandham Hall and how it differed from Leo's life at home.

R. L. STEVENSON: *Dr Jekyll and Mr Hyde*
Describe the change in Dr Jekyll's life after the murder of Sir Danvers Carew.

PAPER 3   USE OF ENGLISH   (2 hours)

1 *Fill each of the numbered blanks in the following passage. Use only* **one** *word in each space.*

Isambard Kingdom Brunel was a famous nineteenth-century engineer. He ....(1) born in 1806 in Portsmouth, a seaport in the South of England. In 1823, after studying ....(2) two years in Paris, he started ....(3) for his father, ...(4) was an engineer and inventor. He had been born near Rouen in France but in 1792 had left France for the USA and had later settled in England. Both father and son were responsible for the design ....(5) construction of the first tunnel under the River Thames. The digging of this tunnel was ....(6) in 1825 and completed twenty years later. Today, it ....(7) part of the London Underground system.

Isambard Kingdom Brunel went ....(8) to design the *Great Britain* (1845), ...(9) was the first large ship to be built ....(10) iron instead of wood. It was powered ....(11) steam and made regular crossings of the Atlantic. Remarkably, this ship is ....(12) in existence. It ....(13) been restored and can be seen in Bristol, ...(14) it was originally built. ....(15) of Brunel's great engineering achievements was the construction of the Great Western Railway from London to Bristol. He designed all the stations, bridges, tunnels and viaducts along the line.

Brunel's ideas were ahead of his time and he had difficulty in convincing people that they were realistic, and, indeed, some of his projects were very ambitious, but he ....(16) determined to find ....(17) to the ....(18) difficult problems. Overwork ruined his health and he ....(19), at the early age of fifty-two, in 1859. The work of Brunel,

91

and his father, has always been highly regarded and Brunel University, founded in 1966, is ....(20) after both of them.

2 *Finish each of the following sentences in such a way that it means the same as the sentence printed before it.*

EXAMPLE: I haven't enjoyed myself so much for years.

ANSWER: It's years *since I enjoyed myself so much.*

a) Did they build the garage at the same time as the house?
Was ....

b) The people who were at the meeting will say nothing to the press.
Nobody who ....

c) The heavy rain made it impossible for us to have our picnic.
We were ....

d) Joan will stay on at school unless she finds a good job before September.
If ....

e) I don't really want to go out tonight.
I'd rather ....

f) Shirley didn't begin to read until she was eight.
It wasn't ....

g) Lucy hasn't worn that dress since Barbara's wedding.
The last ....

h) Let's go abroad for our holiday this year.
Why ....

i) He is such a slow speaker that his students get very bored.
He speaks ....

j) Mackenzie wrote four best-sellers before he was twenty.
By the age of twenty ....

3 *Fill each space in the following sentences with* **one** *appropriate word connected with the subject of printed information.*

    EXAMPLE: When he arrived at Heathrow Airport, Grant bought a book entitled 'A Visitor's *Guide* to London'.

a) Elizabeth looked up the word in her ....

b) When he goes to the theatre, he always buys a ....

c) I'll pick up some .... from the travel agent's, and then we can plan our holiday.

d) You can get a free railway .... at the station information office.

e) Their telephone number is not in the ....

4 *Complete these sentences with a phrasal verb that includes the word* **up.**

    EXAMPLES: They bought an old house and *did* it *up.*
                  I'm not going to *put up with* this noise any longer.

a) I don't believe a word of your story. I think you're just .... it *up.*

b) The publication of his new book was .... *up* by a strike.

c) Her party was not a success. She'd been expecting nearly 40 people but only 15 .... *up* and most of them left early.

d) This piece of equipment is very well made and will .... *up* .... the roughest treatment. You won't have any trouble with it.

e) He .... *up* tennis in order to get fit.

5 *Make all the changes and additions necessary to produce, from the following sets of words and phrases, sentences which together make a complete letter. Note carefully from the example what kind of alterations need to be made. Write each sentence in the space provided.*

EXAMPLE: I be very surprised / receive / letter / you this morning.

ANSWER: *I was very surprised to receive a letter from you this morning.*

27 Poets Road
Cambridge

5 December 1989

The Personnel Officer
Cantab Export Ltd
1 Hill Street
Cambridge
CB1 2EU

Dear Sir,

I write / reply / your advertisement / yesterday's *Evening Guardian.*

a) ....

In it you say / you look / secretary / good typing skills who be fluent / French / English.

b) ....

I just complete / two-year bilingual secretarial course / my local college.

c) ....

At / end / course I pass all / exams / good marks.

d) ....

Before I start it / I spend / year / France / living / French family.

e) ....

While I be there / I l arn / speak French fluently.

f) ....

I be very grateful / you send me more information about / job / application form.

g) ....

I look forward / hear / you.

h) ....

Yours faithfully,

Janet Waters

6 *At Meadowlands International College, all students have the opportunity to take part in a variety of activities. Below you will find information about some of these activities and teachers' comments about three of the students, Isobel, Mauro and Thomas. Decide which activities these three students are likely to choose and give your reasons. Write your answers in the spaces provided on page 96.* **(You do not need to use all the information.)**

COLLEGE NOTICE BOARD

URGENT!!!

We're preparing an information pack for new students. Advice on shops, discos, restaurants, bars, cinemas, theatres — places to go, things to do, where to meet people.

Help needed to get up-to-date information. Serious research — but lots of fun (and late nights) too!

Interested? Contact Liza or Philip NOW!

HELP!

I'm drowning in paper, tapes, books, magazines — trying to reorganise Meadowlands library.
Can you help me? Good planning skills essential!

Contact Julian in Room B37 anytime.

Brookfield Home for the Elderly

Spare a thought for the old and lonely! Join our visiting group now! We go to Brookfield twice a week and organise activities, singing, dancing etc. for the old people there. They love it and you'll hear lots of stories about what life was like years ago.

Meet in the coffee bar Tuesday 8 p.m. to find out more.

ENJOY THE MAGIC OF THE MOUNTAINS

Co-driver needed for minibus for week's trip to Scotland.
Camping, walking, some climbing.
Share expenses. Meet new people, make new friends. Leaving Monday.

Meet in Room G17 7.30 p.m. this Saturday.

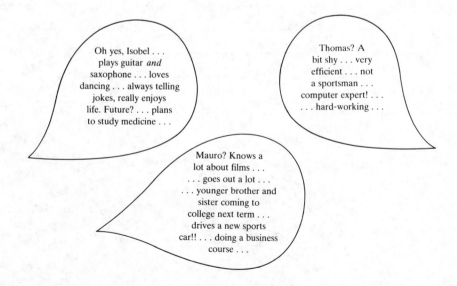

Oh yes, Isobel . . . plays guitar *and* saxophone . . . loves dancing . . . always telling jokes, really enjoys life. Future? . . . plans to study medicine . . .

Thomas? A bit shy . . . very efficient . . . not a sportsman . . . computer expert! . . . . . . hard-working . . .

Mauro? Knows a lot about films . . . . . . goes out a lot . . . . . . younger brother and sister coming to college next term . . . drives a new sports car!! . . . doing a business course . . .

I think Thomas ....

....

....

....

....

....

....

I expect Isobel ....

....

....

....

....

....

....

....

Mauro ....

....

....

....

....

....

....

....

PAPER 4 LISTENING COMPREHENSION
(about 30 minutes)

PART ONE

You will hear two sisters discussing their father's illness. For questions 1 to 4 tick one of the boxes A, B, C or D to show the correct answer.

1 The first sister complains because she

A is afraid of becoming exhausted.

B can't give enough attention to her father.

C feels ill with worry.

D is finding the situation very difficult.

A	
B	
C	
D	

2 The other sister wants their father to go to hospital because she thinks that

A he is not happy at home.

B he would get better more quickly.

C he is not aware of his surroundings.

D they could visit him at weekends.

A	
B	
C	
D	

3 The first sister becomes upset because she thinks her sister is

A lazy.

B unfeeling.

C pessimistic.

D critical.

A	
B	
C	
D	

4 The situation is difficult for Robert because he

   A doesn't have many friends.

   B doesn't like his father-in-law.

   C has to stay at home.

   D enjoys his job.

A	
B	
C	
D	

PART TWO

You will hear a woman talking about things she wants for her new kitchen. For questions 5 to 14, tick the boxes next to the items of equipment which she wants. Leave the other boxes blank.

5 an extra sink ☐

6 a freezer ☐

7 a fridge ☐

8 an ice-cream maker ☐

9 a gas hob ☐

10 a gas oven ☐

11 a microwave oven ☐

12 a lamp ☐

13 open shelves ☐

14 wall cupboards ☐

PART THREE

You will hear some announcements being made in a department store. For questions 15 to 24 fill in the missing information in the picture of the shop window below.

PAPER 5 INTERVIEW (about 15 minutes)

You will be asked to take part in a theme-directed conversation with the examiner. You may be by yourself, with another candidate or with two other candidates. (Two examiners are present when there are three candidates.) The conversation will be based on one particular topic area, for example holidays, work, food.

A typical interview is described below.

★ You will be shown one, two or three photographs and invited to talk about them.

★ The examiner will then show you one or more passages and invite you to link them to the theme. You may be asked to talk a little about the content of the passage. You will *not*, however, be asked to read the passage aloud but you may quote parts of it to make your point.

★ You will then be asked to take part in a communicative activity with the other candidates present and/or the examiner (or examiners). This could involve role-play, problem solving, planning, rank ordering etc. or it could be a discussion on another aspect of the general theme of the conversation. Advertisements, diagrams and other realia are often used as stimuli here.

You will find six sample First Certificate interviews at the back of this book. Your teacher can help you to prepare for this part of the examination by assuming the role of the examiner and telling you which item in the Interview Exercises you should look at.

Interview Exercises

PRACTICE TEST 1

FAMILY AND FRIENDS

1

2

3

4 Me? I'd hate to have a twin. Just imagine having someone who looked just like you, talked like you and probably dressed like you! How could you feel like your*self* with your double walking around!!

5 Well, I come from a family of seven children and I'm glad because when I was young I had brothers and sisters around to help me. Even if I didn't get along with one there were plenty of others. But we did have some hard times with so many mouths to feed.

6 My best friend and I are even closer than sisters. We do everything together, talk about everything. I can't talk to my own sister at all. But then, she's six years older than me.

7 *The qualities we look for in a friend*
 – a sense of humour
 – loyalty
 – honesty
 – agreeing with everything you say
 – hard working
 – having the same interests as you
 – good looks
 – patience
 – intelligence
 – skill at sports

8 **Role A** You borrowed your brother's (sister's) cassette player without asking and accidentally broke it. Have a talk with him (her) about it.

 Role B Your brother (sister) borrowed your cassette player without asking and broke it. Have a talk with him (her) about it.

 Role C Your son (daughter) borrowed his (her) brother's (sister's) cassette player without asking and broke it. Have a talk with your children about it.

9 You may be invited to discuss the following:

An only child is a lonely child.

Blood is thicker than water.

It's better to have one really good friend than lots of acquaintances.

PRACTICE TEST 2

THE SEA

10

S/S Heimdall, trafikerande linjen Stockholm-Åbo året runt.   Stockholms Rederi AB. Svea.

11

12

13 That's something I've always wanted to try. It looks so easy when you watch someone doing it, but I guess you need a pretty good sense of balance.

14 Once out on the open sea the men began to relax and enjoy it. There was just enough breeze to get up a good speed but not enough to make the sea too rough. The sun shone down out of a cloudless blue sky. It was a perfect day for sailing.

15 Here she comes now! Thank goodness the supplies will be here before the winter. Another week or so and no ships will get in or out of here.

16 You may be invited to discuss what you imagine to be the good and bad points of some of the following:

being a fisherman living by the sea
being a deep-sea diver a holiday by the sea
being a beach life-guard going on a long cruise
being in the navy

17

FANTASTIC! FABULOUS!

FIRST PRIZE

FREE!

Holiday on the Sea
- for 4 people
- for 4 weeks
- anywhere in the world

Yachting   Surfing   Swimming   sailing   diving

Sunbathing

Imagine you have won first prize in a competition. The prize is a free holiday on the sea for four people, for four weeks, anywhere in the world.

Discuss and decide

- what kind of holiday you would choose (relaxing, active, sports)
- who you would take with you and why
- where you would go
- what you would take with you (e.g. food, radio, maps, clothes etc.)
- how you would spend your time

PRACTICE TEST 3

THE MEDIA

18

19

20

21 I wish she would turn the radio down. All we hear from morning till night is music and news bulletins. The sound travels right through the walls in this place and we never have a minute's peace.

22 Excuse me! Do you think I could borrow your newspaper if you've finished with it? I didn't have time to buy one at the station this morning. I hope you don't mind me asking.

Discuss

23 I don't know why you watch that rubbish on the TV. I can't stand it myself. There must be something more interesting than that on surely! And if there isn't, just switch it off and do something useful.

24

IF YOU WANT TO KNOW HOW LONG THEY WATCH T.V. - COUNT THE RINGS ROUND THEIR EYES

25

Channel 1		Channel 2		Channel 3		Channel 4	
8.00pm	**Bread** More comedy with the hilarious family from Liverpool	8.00pm	**Wildlife in Tasmania** Nature documentary	8.00pm	**Football** Albania v. England Live coverage of the whole of this World Cup qualifying match from Tirana	8.00pm	**Happy Days** Classic American comedy series
8.30pm	**By Bike Across China** Travel documentary	9.00pm	**News**			8.30pm	**The Sound of Music** A romantic musical film based on a real life story in wartime Austria
9.30pm	**World War II** Part 10. Continuing this important history series	9.30pm	**News EXTRA** Discussion of current issues	10.00pm	**News**		
10.00pm	**News**	10.00pm	**Sportsnight**			10.00pm	**News**

PRACTICE TEST 4

SPORT

26

27

28

29 'What an experience! We never thought we'd see sportsmen like that in real life – something to tell everyone at home about. They must have to train 24 hours a day!'

30 Manchester United manager Alex Ferguson last night tipped Norwich to claim the League title. He took his team home from East Anglia after a 2–1 defeat saying 'Norwich are good enough to go all the way.'

31 Past Glories is now completely fit again after recovering from a leg injury sustained last summer. He has had several good gallops recently, but I am more impressed by the form of Fu's Lady. She should win on Saturday, with Silver Ace a close second.

You may be asked to suggest the most suitable sports or physical activities for some or all of the following people:
a) a retired person, reasonably fit, has a lot of free time
b) a housewife would like to take up an activity while her young children are at nursery school
c) a middle-aged businessman, overweight and with very little free time, wants to get fit
d) a student wants to do something energetic and to meet people – something competitive perhaps

33   The benefits of doing daily exercise.

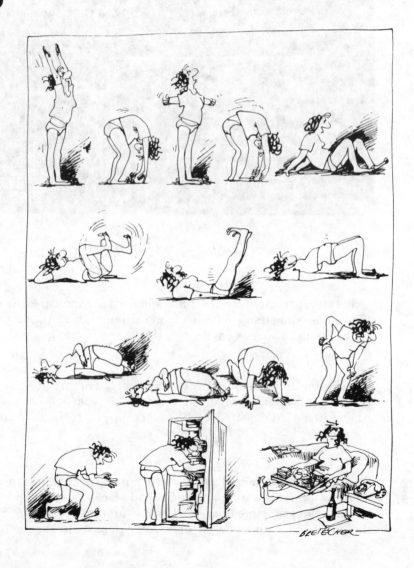

PRACTICE TEST 5

COMMUNITY SPIRIT

34

35

36

37 Let The People Sing – at school, at church, in the street, in the home. Wherever people are, however bad things are, singing together makes life better, brings us all closer.

38 Spring 1989 Programme
We are a small but friendly group simply trying to enjoy life and help others to do the same. We have been in existence since 1932 and are always willing to welcome new members, no matter what age or nationality.

   So why not come along to one of our regular events this week or phone one of our Committee Members TODAY!

39 We love the tea room at the centre. It's somewhere you can go and have a chat and a laugh. Stops you feeling lonely, I can tell you!

40

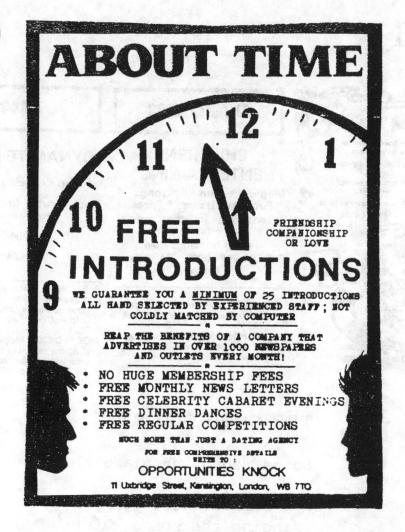

You may be asked to talk about this Friendship Agency.

41

ADAM ANT

The Best Childrens
entertainment

Fun, Magic, Puppets,
Games.

Full catering service
available.

Call now for special rates.

91-851 4185.

You may be asked to plan an evening for
a) a group of 6–10 year old children
and/or b) a group of 16 year olds
and/or c) a group of old people

OPTIONAL READING

L P HARTLEY: *The Go-Between*

42

43

*Atropa
Belladonna*

44

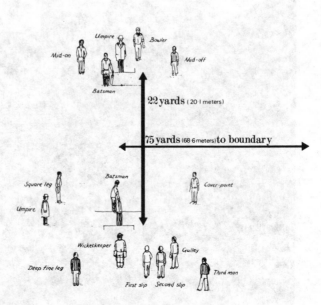

These are the main positions on the cricket field.

45

I should have been ashamed of those curses because they were wrong, even wicked, perhaps. But I was not ashamed of them then and I am not ashamed of them now. Indeed, I envy the strength of character that I used to have. When I was young, I did not turn away from my enemies. I used to fight them my own way.

46 I now began to enjoy the hot weather. I liked to feel the heat on my skin. The green suit was made of thin cloth and it had an open neck. My trousers were also open at the knee. My new stockings were hardly thick enough to protect my legs from thorns. But I was especially proud of my new shoes, partly because they were just like Marcus's.

47 I stood up and walked about. My knee was beginning to feel better. I was already planning the story that I should tell at Brandham Hall. But I owed something to the farmer. I would not have offered him money even if I had had any. But perhaps I could give him a present. I looked around the bare kitchen. I wondered whether he needed anything.

48 I decided, then, to read it. There were other good arguments in my favour. This letter might be the last that I should deliver. If it was very secret or very important, I would probably carry more in spite of Marcus's presence. If Marian was in danger, she would expect me to read it.

49 I stretched out my hand and touched the flowers and leaves. They held my hand. If I went inside the hut, I should learn its secret. And it would learn mine. I went in. It was hot and soft and comfortable inside. A flower touched my face. Some of the fruit rubbed against my lips . . .

50 Mrs Maudsley said nothing. She ran with wide, awkward steps, and her skirt was dragging through the mud. It was soon clear that she was guiding me. She knew where we were going. When we came to the path between the bushes, I tried to turn her back.

I cried, 'Not this way, Mrs Maudsley!'

≫→

51 You will be asked to talk about one or more of the following topics:

1 Country house life in 1900

2 Mrs Maudsley

3 Leo's relationship with Ted Burgess

4 The problems of adolescence

5 Lord Trimingham

6 Your general impressions of the book